NO MORE

unshackle your heart and your mind

LIES

JILL TOMLINSON

Carpenter's Son Publishing

CONTENTS

ENDORSEMENTS

I meet people every day who are suffering under a load of guilt, shame, fear and worthlessness—all because they have believed lies. In her new book *No More Lies*, Jill Tomlinson takes a sledgehammer to the lies that paralyze us. Using the truth of God's Word, she dismantles the most common strategies of our common enemy. If you or someone you love is struggling to get free, I strongly recommend this book.

J. Lee Grady
Former Editor, Charisma *Magazine*
Author, 10 Lies the Church Tells Women *and* The Holy Spirit Is Not for Sale

If your past has held you captive to feelings of worthlessness and inferiority, then *No More Lies* is for you! Jill has done an excellent job of exposing the lies of the enemy and society that keep so many from realizing their full potential in Christ. Her testimony of victory in spite of the heartbreaking events in her early life is truly inspiring. Let the Holy Spirit minister to you through the pages of this wonderful book!

Barry Bennett
Dean of Students
Charis Bible College

DEDICATION

This book is dedicated to the following:

THE LOVER OF MY SOUL, JESUS CHRIST

You miraculously turned my ashes to beauty, my mourning to dancing, and You continue to love me with an everlasting, unrelenting love. You are my Everything.

MY HUSBAND AND BEST FRIEND, JIMMY

God has used you in my life in powerful ways. You have been a conduit for His love, healing, and encouragement to flow into my life. We have been on mountaintops, and we have walked through valleys. Through it all, I am thankful we are walking through this life hand in hand. Your steadfast support throughout the writing of this book has been amazing to me. I love you.

MY CHILDREN, ASHLEY, IVEY, AND CONNOR, AND MY NEW SON-IN-LOVE, PATRICK

I have been your teacher, mom, mentor, and friend, but I have learned much more from you than you will ever imagine. You are my heart, and I love you more than words can ever express. Thank you for your selflessness and encouragement throughout the days and months it took for me to write this book. You are all world-changers, destined for mighty works that were ordained for you before the foundations of this world. May you always walk in the truth of who your Father God says you are. I love you with all that I am, but He loves you even more. You are His, and He is faithful.

MY PARENTS AND FAMILY

Thank you for loving me through the dark days of my life all those years ago. I am so proud to be your daughter and your sister. The enemy meant much harm to our family, but God has blessed us with a rich heritage of love and grace from His royal throne. I love you all more than you will ever know. A special thanks to my mom who spent countless hours proofreading my manuscript. You are a treasure, and I am blessed to be your daughter.

MY PASTOR, MENTOR, AND FRIEND, STEVE COMER

Thank you for believing in me when I didn't believe I could ever be usable, for showing me God's unconditional love, and for being a man of integrity even in the face of pain and persecution. Your life and your ministry are powerful, and you have made an eternal impact on my life.

TO THE ONE OR THE MANY FOR WHOM THIS BOOK WAS WRITTEN

You are deeply loved, called by name, and purposefully chosen. May you see yourself and your life as your Father God sees you.

INTRODUCTION

He is called the "Great Deceiver" for a reason. You see, the lies begin early, and they do not stop, but instead they compound. One lie builds upon the next, and for every lie that Satan subtly whispers, another waits in the shadows to solidify the one before. Each lie is as a chain wrapped around the soul, binding and choking the very life within.

This book is not an autobiography. My testimony, however, is a graphic representation of how powerful the deception of Satan can be. I share some of my most innermost thoughts and weaknesses in the following paragraphs so you will realize how I am able to speak of the topics within this book. This introduction includes a brief, but very personal, glimpse into the depths of some of the darkest days of my life, and my subsequent journey into the arms of God.

My story begins when I was only three or four years old. It is almost impossible to believe that a child not much older than a toddler can be attacked by satanic lies, yet it happens. It happened to me. My first memories are those of explicit sexual abuse by an extended family member. I was told this would be a "fun game." Immediately I knew it was like no other game I had ever played and that something was very wrong, but

I felt powerless to do anything. I believed the lie that these disgusting acts were my fault and that I was just as guilty as my perpetrator. Although I didn't know the word for it at the time, I was introduced to shame at this point in my life.

The toxicity of the lie of shame cannot be emphasized enough. It is the lie that kept me silent for many agonizing years. I honestly believed I was to blame. Even as young as I was, Satan convinced me I was worthless. I was molested not once, but repeatedly, during the next few years as a result of this lie. It kept me in fear and prevented me from revealing the ugliness that was happening until I could no longer carry the heavy load alone. Finally, at the age of seven, I painfully told my family about this horrible "secret" that had imprisoned my young life.

Although I didn't come close to telling my family everything I had been through, I can remember being almost frozen in place with complete humiliation and disgust for myself. I saw the looks of pain and disdain on the faces of my family and wished I could just evaporate. Later in my life, I realized the looks that I saw that night were anguish for the trauma I had suffered and anger toward my perpetrator. They were not indicative of rejection toward me. However, at the time I believed the lie that I was a huge disappointment to those who loved me. In my mind full of self-accusation, my confession had ruined their day. I felt filthy. I was convinced they saw me for what I already believed I was: dirty and useless. This was another life-altering lie I believed; I thought I was no longer lovable.

After that dark night when I disclosed my secret, I concluded that everything was different. Satan convinced me that my parents and siblings saw me in a different light. I believed the false accusation from the enemy that I was no longer their innocent baby, but a burden and embarrassment. This lie was whispered in my ear constantly. It was always there nagging at me and weighing on my heart. I erroneously felt indescribably different from everyone else. To intensify this feeling, I truly believed I was pregnant for many years but was afraid to tell anyone. I was locked in the prison of my own thoughts and lies that Satan fed me day after day after day. I had unknowingly become the target of a vicious attack from an enemy I didn't even know I had.

Miraculously, I accepted Jesus into my heart as a young girl. I look back at the way He pursued me with His gentle love, and I am amazed. I had always loved Him, since I could remember, and felt that He had His hand upon me in some strange way. I didn't understand everything about the Christian faith, nor did I need to. I just wanted Jesus in my heart. It was a simple yet most profound decision. I carried my pocket Bible to school and spent recess and free time proudly sharing God's love and message of salvation. Despite the abuse and the lies, I was not shy or quiet. I was bold and outgoing, and I was using it for my Savior. Meanwhile, however, I was still plagued with fiery darts and self-doubt. As my adversary would have it, I tucked each lie deep inside and lived in the silent hell he was creating. Although I had made the decision to give my life to Jesus, my mind was not renewed to the truth of

God's Word. I never realized what was happening, but Satan was gaining control of my thoughts.

As I grew older, the lies intensified even as my love for the Lord increased. I began to fall for the lie that I could never measure up to those around me because I was different; I was "dirty." Satan was ready and waiting in the shadows for an opportunity to snatch me into the pits of darkness. He had been setting me up my whole life for the snares that he was laying before me. Even though I was zealous for the Lord, I had very little revelation of His love for me. I wasn't prepared to withstand the temptations, and I was an easy target. I foolishly and unassumingly, one by one, stepped into each snare he laid, and I suffered greatly as a result.

The years that followed included unspeakable heartache and pain including destructive relationships, scarring betrayal, an unwed pregnancy, an abusive marriage, divorce, alcohol abuse, and a long line of bad decisions followed by painful consequences. I became my own worst enemy as my torment increased, and I made choices based on my fear instead of God's truth. I caused anguish not only to myself, but also to people in my life whom I loved deeply. I mistakenly came to believe that trust was for the weak or ignorant. As a result, I began to live a life of emotional isolation.

Satan's grip on me became increasingly more intense with each bad choice that I made. My life began to spiral out of control. Every sin and lie made me feel farther from the caring arms of my Heavenly Father until I became convinced that God would never love me again. So, like Adam and Eve in the Garden of Eden, I ran and tried to hide my shame from God.

Just as I was about to begin my first year of college, I found out I was pregnant. I had been in an unhealthy relationship for nearly a year. Although marriage seemed to be the best solution to "cover" my sin, the thought of it terrified me. I chose to remain single. During the difficult days of my pregnancy, many efforts were made by well-intentioned people to make me aware of the option of abortion. Thank God, He never stopped trying to lovingly direct my path. Something inside me rose up against the thought. Abortion was never an option in my heart or mind. The abortion that I refused to have is now a beautiful 22-year-old young woman with a passionate heart for God. She is and has been a very real reminder to me of God's grace and mercy. Although I was unaware at the time, God had not forsaken me.

Abortion will be discussed further in a later chapter, but if you have had an abortion or have been the partner of someone who has, you need to know right now that there is forgiveness. I have ministered to people who have had multiple abortions and believed there was no hope of forgiveness. Jesus paid the price. DO NOT believe the lie that you cannot be forgiven, that you have gone too far, or that you are not loved!

Even after the miraculous birth of my daughter, the lies continued to consume my thoughts and alter my decisions. I felt used and unworthy. My dream had always been to marry a Christian man who loved God passionately. Feelings of regret and condemnation were overwhelming. How had my life turned out so opposite from the thing I wanted it to be? How could I have become so very different from the person I yearned in my heart to become?

I vividly remember finally coming to the place of believing that if, by chance, *anyone* came along who would want to marry me, I should consider it a blessing. What a poisonous lie! Before long someone did come along, and, without consulting God, I married him. My misery intensified. This relationship and the abuse it entailed confirmed what Satan had whispered all of my life: I was not worth loving. After two agonizing years, I walked away feeling more broken, confused, and worthless than ever before.

By 21 years old, I was at an all-time low in my life. Through all the pain, I became quite resilient. I put up whatever walls were necessary to survive. I intended to make a safe life for my daughter, even if I did it alone. Little did I know I was not alone—ever. Even in the midst of bad choices, confusion, agony, and disappointment, God had a purpose for my life. His mercy continued to follow me, even though I was unaware.

By God's grace, I have now been married to a wonderful man with a heart like King David for 19 years. We have a beautiful, blessed family. Our three amazing children are full of personality, passion, and purpose. According to this world's standards, I am not a qualified or worthy recipient, yet the Lord graciously orders my steps. I have loved every minute of being a mom, and I determined from the beginning to teach my children about the Lord's love for them. All the while, though, I believed it was too late for me. My goal in life became to make sure they didn't make the same mistakes I had made.

Even as I was being showered with blessings from the Lord, I remained bound, blindfolded, and spiritually and emotionally sick. Although I learned to "function" in it, I became very accustomed to my prison. I was quiet and withdrawn with anyone outside the family. I was not this way because I had nothing to say, but because I was convinced that nothing that came from me could be of any use to anyone else. I was constantly reminded of all the bad choices I had made and that I wasn't worthy to do anything for anyone, especially the Lord. I found that I was in my comfort zone when I was unnoticed. I didn't want to be this way, but I literally felt paralyzed with fear and shame. My heart broke over and over again—for I was no longer the bold little girl with a message. Instead, I had become withdrawn and untouchable. The lies went on and on.

Everything changed when I came face to face with death. While on vacation, I had a severe allergic reaction to an antibiotic. I literally felt the talons of death around me in the moments that followed in the ambulance. After that initial reaction, I remained very ill, and for nearly a year, I continued to experience debilitating symptoms of a severe allergic reaction. I was in and out of hospitals and doctors offices. After many months, no concrete answers were found. Still, there remained a myriad of symptoms for which I was prescribed 14 or 15 different medications to control. With very little strength to even get back and forth to the bathroom some days, I spent many hours in bed questioning the Lord and feeling I had finally gotten what I deserved. I quickly realized a spiritual battle was being waged for my very life.

One morning as I fought for the breath to dress myself, I nearly collapsed in my closet. In desperation, I cried out to God, unsure if He would hear me. By this time, I was convinced that if I had even ever had it at all, my salvation was gone. I knew, however, that my only hope of surviving was God. Doctors couldn't figure it out and I couldn't figure it out, but I knew that God was keenly aware of what was happening in my body. I realized that He alone was my Healer and my only hope. That morning I repented for the pathetic life I had lived, and I put my life and fate in the hands of the Lord. He met me in a miraculous way. Although physically I felt nothing spectacular or different at the moment, my heart changed. I fully and completely emptied myself of me, and I put myself in the hands of the Almighty. In the days that followed, one by one, my symptoms began to subside. Within a few short weeks, I was able to come off all medications, and I was supernaturally restored to health. Praise His Name!!

For years prior to this experience, my husband and I had been in and out of church. I despised religion and still do because it is lifeless, full of unattainable law, and has nothing at all to do with a relationship with Jesus Christ. In fact, it is just the opposite of everything that an intimate relationship with Jesus is all about. It was the religious people of the day who fought Jesus so vehemently. They were more concerned with their own images and the traditions of men than they were about truth and life. Truly there are plenty of Pharisees and Sadducees still around today, but I thought that *every* church was about dead religion and fake, hypocritical people. This was a lie that kept me from the Body of Christ and from hearing the truth proclaimed—truth that held the power to set me free.

Shortly after my encounter with the Lord in my closet that day, we found a church home. It was so good to be in the house of the Lord. My husband and I were facing monumental financial loss and found our way to the altar for prayer. I will never forget feeling the love of God flow through our pastor as he put his hands on each of us to pray. Never before had I felt the love of God in such a tangible way. I will always thank God for my pastor. It was through him at many different times and in many different ways that I saw my first glimpses of what the love of my Heavenly Father looked like.

On another occasion, I went to the altar and began begging God the way I usually did. It's all I knew. Even after He had healed me and touched me with His love, I felt completely unworthy to approach Him. In an instant, however, my life changed forever. It was as if someone removed blindfolds from my eyes. My life, from my earliest and ugliest memories, flashed before me and every lie was exposed. In that moment, I saw clearly what had been happening in the spirit realm as I watched the movie of my life play before me. It was the most profound moment of my life. I remember repeatedly speaking aloud, "It has all been lies!" I literally fell on my face before the Lord and repented for accepting the deception my whole life. I basked in the presence and goodness of God. That night my life truly began. It was the beginning of my love story with the Lord. It was then that the message for this book was seared in my heart.

Since that time, I have never looked back. While there have been moments and seasons of discouragement, there has never been a temptation to turn from the God who gave me life. He is everything to me. He is the very life that sustains me.

Following that cloud nine experience, I realized that an average day in the Christian life is not as surreal. Instead, it is a minute by minute, day by day faith in God. Never be discouraged by a lack of chill bumps. While supernatural encounters with Him are wonderful, real, and needed, the intimate daily walk with Him is where victory lies. It is the one true relationship that far surpasses human feelings.

In the days and months that followed, the Holy Spirit taught me and led me into a place of liberty and peace that I had never known before. The remainder of this book contains many of the powerful truths God used in my life as He lovingly guided me into this place of utter deliverance and freedom. It has been a journey of discovery, healing, and unspeakable joy.

I have shared this very personal portion of my testimony with you, and I share the life-changing truths in the remainder of this book with the sincere prayer that other captives will be made free. May the words on each page bring revelation and point you to the One who has enough love to cover any wound, any sin, and any pain. His love is a healing balm—let it flow over your soul like honey and expose every lie, heal every hurt, and bring forth all truth and knowledge of your Maker and the Lover of your soul.

chapter 1

YOUR FATHER'S EYES

And you shall know the truth,
and the truth shall make you free. ~ John 8:32

HOME, SWEET HOME

The lies of the enemy are subtle, often taking root over a period of years without notice. They may be small, nearly undetectable mindsets that you have had since childhood. However, *any* mindset, regardless of how insignificant it may seem, that is contrary to the Word of God will negatively influence your life, decisions, and relationships.

Every person was created by God. The first time anyone saw you with physical eyes was on an ultrasound machine or in a delivery room. What they were not able to see was where you came from. I do not refer to the obvious physical events that took place in bringing about your physical existence, but to the spiritual origination of the person who looks back at you in the mirror. Your home originated in the heart of your Heavenly Father, long before you ever had an earthly one.

How blessed is God! And what a blessing he is! He's the Father of our Master, Jesus Christ, and takes us to the high places of blessing in him. Long before he laid down earth's foundations, he had us in mind, had settled on us as the focus of his love, to be made whole and holy by his love. Long, long ago he decided to adopt us into his family through Jesus Christ. (What pleasure he took in planning this!) He wanted us to enter into the celebration of his lavish gift-giving by the hand of his beloved Son (Ephesians 1:3–6 MSG).

This passage vividly describes God's heart for His children! For the purpose of this chapter, see your home as the place where your Heavenly Father first dreamt of you. You say, "God has never had dreams about *me!*" Oh, but He has. As the scripture declares, He carefully purposed you. Regardless of the circumstances surrounding your physical birth, you were *not* an accident. You were planned before time to be His and to be here for such a time as this. He loves you with an everlasting, unrelenting love.

The intent of the enemy of your soul is to lure you away from your true home (the heart of your Father) to a foreign land. The testimony I shared with you in the introduction of this book is a drastic, but true, example of what being drawn away can eventually look like. However, you can be a Bible-believing, churchgoing Christian and wander away in a certain area such as how you think about your spouse, children, parents, co-workers, or others. You can wander or be headed away from home in your attitude about work, money, career, or habits in regards to eating, taking care of your body, or more destructive patterns involving drugs, abusive behavior, anger issues, and more. This list is almost endless. There are many, many ways that the enemy attempts to lure you away with his cunning lies.

As I shared in the introduction, there was a moment in time after many years of aimless wandering when I returned home in a radical way. As I look back over those dark years now, I see how the Lord always gently pursued me with His passionate love. Even in my darkest night, He was there. The enemy never wanted me to see it, and he doesn't want you to see it either, but the realization of God's extravagant, unchanging love will set you free in every area of life. This revelation is a process, as His love is overwhelming.

The following passage of scripture describes someone who came to his senses and returned home to see this love in a powerful way:

Jesus continued: "There was a man who had two sons. The younger one said to his father, 'Father, give me my share of the estate.' So he divided his property between them.

"Not long after that, the younger son got together all he had, set off for a distant country and there

squandered his wealth in wild living. After he had spent everything, there was a severe famine in that whole country, and he began to be in need. So he went and hired himself out to a citizen of that country, who sent him to his fields to feed pigs. He longed to fill his stomach with the pods that the pigs were eating, but no one gave him anything.

*"**When he came to his senses,** he said, 'How many of my father's hired men have food to spare, and here I am starving to death! I will set out and go back to father and say to him: Father, I have sinned against heaven and against you. I am no longer worthy to be called your son; make me like one of your hired men.' So he got up and went to his father.*

"But while he was still a long way off, his father saw him and was filled with compassion for him; he ran to his son, threw his arms around him and kissed him.

"The son said to him, 'Father, I have sinned against heaven and against you. I am no longer worthy to be called your son.'

"But the father said to his servants, 'Quick! Bring the best robe and put it on him. Put a ring on his finger and sandals on his feet. Bring the fattened calf and kill it. Let's have a feast and celebrate. For this son of mine was dead and is alive again; he was lost and is found.' So they began to celebrate." (Luke 15:11–24 NIV, emphasis added)

If you will notice, the father's love had always been there. It was the son who walked away from his father's goodness. The rights of the son could always be found at his father's home: his place at the table, his warm bed, his provision, and protection. At his father's house, he was royalty. These privileges could not be found in a distant land. Yet, the son believed the all too familiar lie that there was something better out there for him, something that he was more deserving of than what he could find at home. He pursued the "greener grass" and lost all that he had.

Once he realized his folly and decided to return home, the son then believed the lie that he had done too much wrong and would have to enter his father's house as a mere servant. He felt unworthy to be called a son. However, the truth was that the father ached for his son's return. When he saw his son coming, he ran to him, embraced him, and rightly restored him as if he had never been gone. The father placed the wayward son right back alongside the faithful, obedient brother who had never left. Neither son was able to comprehend this unconditional love of the father. For differing reasons, it was more than either of them could fathom.

Your Father aches for you. He yearns for you when you go searching for "better" things in distant lands. The goodness of your God cannot be found there. His mercies and royal treatment can only be fully realized when you choose to dwell with Him. He is the most gentle, loving Father, and He will never force you to abide in Him. He will, however, gently pursue you with His love in hopes that you will someday come to your senses and return to His loving arms so He can fully restore you to your rightful places as son or daughter of The Most High God!!

I remember that night when I was still "a long way off" and my Father saw me coming. He ran to me, for I didn't even have the strength to make it all the way home. He wrapped me in His loving arms and carried me to safety. Still, I felt unworthy to be His, and undeserving of being restored as one who had never left. I couldn't comprehend that kind of love. Yet, He removed my clothing of shame, and He covered me in His pure white robe of righteousness. Forevermore, I am His beloved daughter.

If you have been abiding in a distant land, enduring a spiritual famine, He is waiting. Close your eyes for a moment and reflect on your life. Without a doubt, no matter how long you have been gone, or what you have done, He has relentlessly pursued you with His love. Let the Holy Spirit show you how He has gently beckoned you over the years. He aches for you, He treasures you, and He longs to celebrate your homecoming. He yearns for you to realize that your rightful dwelling is with Him and in Him. When He sees you turn toward Him, He will run to you, carry you home, and clothe you in His splendor. He loves you with an everlasting, unquenchable love.

THE TRUTH ABOUT GOD

Seeing God as your loving, compassionate Father is very different from seeing Him as a distant, staunch God who sits in His palace, staring straight ahead with no concern for your menial life. Religious mindsets that are full of traditions of men and empty of relationship with God tell you that you are of no value and that God is virtually untouchable. This could not be further from the truth, yet it keeps many of God's kids at a "safe distance" from Him. His desire is for you to climb up on His lap, talk to Him, and enjoy sweet intimacy with Him.

God is not interested in copycats. He wants you just the way you are. He desires for His relationship with you to look different from the relationship He has with Suzie at church or Joe next door. Just look at all of creation. Nothing is exactly the same as the thing next to it. Not even snowflakes are exactly alike. How much more true should this be for you and your relationship with Him? Let it be unique. It's just between the two of you.

I hope you perceive God's heart of a father toward you and trust Him completely. However, if you were to randomly select 100 people and ask them who they believe God really is and what He is like, you would possibly get 100 different answers. A majority of those answers would likely include words such as judge, good, angry, merciful, loving, wrathful, gracious, giver, and taker. Clearly, many of these descriptions contradict one another. Most of the world and a large majority of the Body of Christ are living in ignorance and confusion as to the true nature of God.

There are unquestionably no greater lies than those about God Himself. While there may be many different doctrines, there is only one truth. Your spiritual victory hangs in the balance of this revelation. If Satan can convince you that God is distant and impersonal, then your relationship with your Father will reflect that belief as you will never feel that your love could be reciprocated. You will guard your heart from the One who so carefully, delicately, and purposefully created you. If you are lured into the false belief that God is authoritative and rigid, you will live in a constant, unhealthy fear of Him and your relationship with Him will be torment. Oppression will bind you as you realize that your efforts to be good enough are futile. If you think God is simply a puppeteer and that everything in the universe happens at His whim, you will be unable to trust Him. As a result, you will never know true intimacy with Him or regard Him as your Source. You cannot base your views of God upon your circumstances, experiences, or narrow window of understanding. You must build an unshakeable foundation of truth.

From the beginning of time, Satan has worked tirelessly to discredit God and His Word. He doesn't have any new tricks, and he is still striving to convince mankind that God is not who He says He is and that His Word is of no value. Much can be learned from Eve's encounter with Satan in the book of Genesis. You can see how your adversary works, and the lengths to which he will go in his attempt to discredit God:

Now the serpent was more cunning than any beast of the field which the Lord God had made. And he said to the woman, "Has God indeed said, 'You shall not eat of every tree of the garden'?"

And the woman said to the serpent, "We may eat the fruit of the trees of the garden; but of the fruit of the tree which is in the midst of the garden, God has said, 'You shall not eat it, nor shall you touch it, lest you die.'"

Then the serpent said to the woman, "You will not surely die. For God knows that in the day you eat of it your eyes will be opened, and you will be like God, knowing good and evil."

So when the woman saw that the tree was good for food, that it was pleasant to the eyes, and a tree desirable to make one wise, she took of its fruit and ate. She also gave to her husband with her, and he ate. Then the eyes of both of them were opened, and they knew that they were naked; and they sewed fig leaves together and made themselves coverings.

And they heard the sound of the Lord God walking in the garden in the cool of the day, and Adam and his wife hid themselves from the presence of the Lord God among the trees of the garden (Genesis 3:1–8).

It did not take the serpent long in this passage of scripture to test Eve's trust in her Creator. Almost immediately, he attempted to get her to question God and what He had really said. Eve must have been wondering if she had really understood the directions from the Lord clearly. Seeds of doubt quickly took root in her mind. Had He really said that they would die? Was He simply keeping the truth from them? In essence, the question Eve was allowing to enter her heart was, "Is God a liar?"

What if Eve had stood fast on the truth of who she knew God to be? After all, she knew Him intimately.

Adam and Eve walked and talked with God regularly. There was no distance between them as they enjoyed sweet fellowship together. Yet, the cunning deception of the serpent was enough to cause her to question the character and trust of her Maker. You know all too well how the rest of the story goes as all mankind suffered tragically at the hand of this one subtle lie.

Truth is truth, whether you choose to believe it and walk in it or not. It never changes. Not unlike Eve, you are bombarded daily with lies and questions about who God really is and whether He truly has good plans for you in mind. Again, you must turn to the Word of God for answers to these questions, and decide in your heart where you will define truth. Will it be in the cunning whispers of the enemy, the empty, powerless words of this world, or the voice of eternal, unchanging truth from the mouth of God?

*But without faith it is impossible to please him: for he that cometh to God must believe that he is, and **that he is a rewarder** of them that diligently seek him (Hebrews 11:6, emphasis added).*

Hebrews 11:6 makes it clear that God is a giver and that it is important to Him that you believe good things about Him. It isn't enough for you to simply believe that He exists. He desires for you to know and believe that He rewards you and desires to give you good things. He wants you to trust Him. Yet, instead, He gets the blame far too often for every tragedy, loss, sickness, hardship, and death. God is not to blame for things the enemy sends your way, for the fallen state of this world, or for those things that your own free will and the will of others directly or indirectly cause. While you can rest in the promise of Romans 8:28, which states that He will make all things work together for your good, He does not necessarily cause or approve of everything you experience on this planet and in your life. Just because He is gracious enough to clean up messes, does not mean He caused things to happen that way in the first place. He loved you enough to give you a free will. He will never override it. That goes contrary to His very nature.

Jesus beautifully modeled His Father's heart in His life and ministry. According to John 5:30, Jesus did nothing of His own accord. He only did those things that were willed by His heavenly Father. Therefore, you can know with certainty that God desires to see captives freed, the oppressed delivered, and the sick and lame healed. Jesus never turned a single person away who was seeking truth, healing, deliverance, or freedom. He never said, "Oh, this infirmity was sent by my Father to make you stronger. You will just need to carry it." He never replied, "I'm sorry, you are not cleaned up enough to come to me today. I think my Father wants to send oppression and suffering upon you instead of setting you free." No! On the contrary, Jesus healed those who were sick, forgave those who were condemned, freed those who were oppressed, and tenderly loosed those who were bound. Scripture tells us that it is the thief (not God) who comes to steal, kill, and destroy!

Then Jesus said to them again, "Most assuredly, I say to you, I am the door of the sheep. All who ever came before Me are thieves and robbers, but the sheep did not hear them. I am the door. If anyone enters by Me, he will be saved, and will go in and out and find pasture. The thief does not come except to steal, and to kill, and to destroy. I have come that they may have life, and that they may have it more abundantly" (John 10:7–10).

Notice in this scripture that Jesus refers to Himself as the door of the sheep—a good Shepherd. Life in Him involves being saved, which is life. The description of going in and out beautifully implies freedom, *not* bondage. Finding pasture describes a life of security, provision, and plenty, not lack, hunger, or constant stress. Can't you just see the description Jesus, according to His Father's will, painted for you in John 10? Can you envision the green, lush grass and the freedom to live an abundant life without worry?

Psalm 23 also depicts a bountiful life, describing provision, peace, and protection. Yet, you face things every single day that are sent to steal, to kill, or to destroy. These things include sickness, financial lack, pain, hopelessness, and a variety of other "gifts" from the enemy. Each day you choose whether to agree with the circumstances you face and embrace them as truth or recognize them for the lies that they are and remind the enemy that he is an imposter! Do not give him place in your life!

As you draw near to God and feed on the ever-growing revelation of His nature, you will experience a greater degree of victory in your life. By agreeing with God, who He is, and who He says you are, you are standing against the enemy. As you submit to God, and resist the lies, Satan will flee (James 4:7). The more you meditate upon God's heart toward you and the abundance He has provided through Christ for every area of your life, the more you experience the abundant life He refers to in John 10:10.

WHAT ABOUT DISCIPLINE?

All too often, discipline is used as the reason for tolerating obstacles in life. When you live with condemnation or you do not understand the true essence of who God is, you decide that any given hardship must be there to discipline you and make you a better person. While the Word is clear that God disciplines those He loves, what is often misinterpreted is the definition of discipline in the eyes of God. True discipline is grounded in love, not anger. Most people associate discipline with harsh punishment, or they see discipline through the eyes of what they have personally seen or experienced. The truth, however, is that God will always guide, shape, and mold you in a loving, gentle way.

According to 2 Timothy 3:16, God uses His word for correction. His Holy Spirit nudges and gently convicts and guides. He is not harsh. He is supremely gentle, yet full of power. He has no need to resort to using tools of the enemy such as sickness, poverty, or other calamity to chastise His children. Would you use a sledgehammer to discipline your child? Of course you wouldn't, and neither would your Heavenly Father use a destructive weapon to correct you! He loves you more than you can imagine and His discipline will only reflect that love.

I think the greatest depiction of God in all the Bible comes from 1 Corinthians 13. As you read the passage below, remember that according to 1 John 4:8–9, God *is* love itself.

> *Love suffers long and is kind; love does not envy; love does not parade itself, is not puffed up; does not behave rudely, does not seek its own, is not provoked, thinks no evil; does not rejoice in iniquity, but rejoices in the truth; bears all things, believes all things, hopes all things, endures all things. Love never fails.* (1 Corinthians 13:4–8)

This passage is often used as a standard of conduct. As you allow God to live through you more and more, this will certainly come to pass in your life. Today, however, I would like you to remember that since God *is* love, you can interject His name in this passage for a powerful glimpse of who He really is:

> *God is patient and kind. He is never boastful, puffed up, envious, or rude. He is not easily provoked. God bears all things, believes all things, hopes all things, and endures all things. He will never, ever fail you.*

Test your ideas about God against these truths. Do your beliefs line up with His goodness? He is always good, loving, kind, compassionate, merciful, and giving. Is that how you see Him through the eyes of your understanding?

I wonder today what you believe in the depths of your heart when it comes to God. Is He your loving Father who picks you up and sets you on His knee?

Does He dance over you? Is He pleased with you? Can you really believe these things about Him? If the answer is anything but "Yes!" then you have accepted a lie somewhere in your heart about who God really is. Pray to the God of love and goodness and ask Him to reveal to you where this seed has been planted and let the light of His truth and love uproot it and replace it with the revelation that you are His everything, and that He would move heaven and earth for you to believe it. God, His goodness, and His nature are the same yesterday, today, and forever (Hebrews 13:8). The goodness and faithfulness of God have never and will never depend upon your circumstances, performance, or perfection.

May grace (God's favor) and peace (which is perfect well-being, all necessary good, all spiritual prosperity, and freedom from fears and agitating passions and moral conflicts) be multiplied to you in [the full, personal, precise, and correct] knowledge of God and of Jesus our Lord (2 Peter 1:2 AMP).

Did you know that God's grace and peace can actually be multiplied to you as you grow in the true knowledge of Him? Meditate today on His goodness and His nature of love. Let it flow like water into the dry, cracked ground deep within your heart. He wants nothing less than all of you. The showers of His love and grace will bring forth new growth, good fruit, and a bountiful life of true joy. He waits with arms open wide. Dance with Him in the healing rain of His goodness, mercy, and tenderness.

chapter 2

GOD IS NOT A PIMP

There is neither Jew nor Greek, there is neither slave nor free, there is neither male nor female; for you are all one in Christ Jesus. ~ Galatians 3:28

CREATED WITH PURPOSE

You read that God is your good and loving Father in the first chapter. Now, take a look at something He is often accused of being, but that He certainly is *not*. The title of this chapter is in no way meant to be offensive or disrespectful. It is only meant to effectively expose an incorrect mindset. Whether you are bold enough to use this terminology or not, there are *many* men and women who inadvertently believe this lie about God. Deep in their hearts they believe that He is less interested in women than men. There are many who believe that He places little value on women, and that they are insignificant to this world and the Body of Christ. Like it or not, this distorted mentality is saying that God is the equivalent of a pimp, and I unknowingly believed it for years.

Written to both men and women, this chapter will powerfully expose and uproot subtle lies targeted at women, their ill treatment, and the lies that both sexes have believed for generations. In this moment, may your heart and mind be open to clearly hear His voice.

Whether it is neglect in an oppressive marriage, being prohibited from ministering in the Body of Christ, or outright verbal or physical abuse, the debasement of women is still very much alive and well. This mindset was not birthed in the throne room of God, but through seeds of deception sown by Satan in the hearts and minds of men and women. These seeds have been growing, multiplying, and taking deeper and deeper root since the fall of Adam and Eve. In these last days, it is more important than ever before that these distorted ideas be brought to light and replaced with truth. As these lies are rejected and truth is implemented, individuals and marriages will be healed, and the Church will be empowered as never before in the history of mankind.

God's intent for relationship with you has always been about intimacy. When you make it anything else—rules, formulas, mundane traditions—you cheapen what God has for you. Jesus endured the cross so you could be restored to an intimate, one-on-one relationship with your Father that had been lost as a result of sin.

Someday, all the fluff will be gone. The only thing that will be left on the day you stand face to face with Jesus is your relationship with Him and the things that have flowed directly out of that relationship. That, beloved, makes it a topic worthy of sincere attention. The deception of the enemy, however, is subtle and always carries with it the purpose of discrediting the Word of God. This is usually accomplished by Satan devaluing you as God's beloved son or daughter.

For many years, a large part of my own deception was the belief that I, as a woman, was of very little value to God or man. I thought that women were merely an afterthought of God. After all, wasn't Eve created for Adam because he was lonely? I can remember asking God many times in my life, "Why did You even create women?" I concluded we were objects, even to Him. After all, that is what experience had told me. Something didn't resonate with my spirit, though. I hungered for the truth about God's heart for women. As I pursued answers, the Lord took me back to the Garden of Eden to begin to show me His truth.

Then God said, "Let us make man in Our image, according to Our likeness; let them have dominion over the fish of the sea, over the birds of the air, and over the cattle, over all the earth, and over every creeping thing that creeps along the ground." So God created man in his own image, in the image of God he created him; male and female he created them (Genesis 1:26–27, emphasis added).

You can see from these scriptures that not only was woman *not* an afterthought, but that the whole Trinity was involved in the planning and creation of *both* genders. While this may seem very foundational to some, for others I hope truth is becoming revelation. It is a powerful realization that "man," being *both* male and female, was carefully, purposefully formed in the image of God. Men and women alike are the crowning glory of God's creation.

There are no afterthoughts with God. There are no sub-standard humans. It's these vague deceptions that create encumbrances in your walk with the Lord, or keep you from ever coming into relationship with Him at all. Why would you want intimacy with someone who never placed value on you? You wouldn't! Satan knows you wouldn't, which is why he works so hard to make you believe it.

Scripture clearly indicates that woman was always part of the plan. She was included in the blueprints of Creation to co-rule with man. She was hand made in the beautiful image of God in His perfect way and timing. While there are definite fundamental differences between men and women, in both design and function, there is absolutely *no* distinction in worth.

USABLE TO GOD

The realization of my worth to God was huge for me, and it intensified my desire to search for keys. I continued to study women of the Bible in my search for answers. As I embarked on my journey into the Word, I saw a beautiful pattern. God used the ordinary and sometimes less than desirable men *and* women to accomplish His divine purposes. He treated the women I read about with love and tenderness. They were clearly not objects to Him, but they were in stark contrast, His treasures.

You are probably familiar with Sarah, the beautiful wife of the great patriarch Abraham. She is an example of a woman who was used mightily by God. Now known as the Mother of Israel, Sarah was barren most of her life. Her pilgrimage with Abraham was quite a journey, and she must have been a strong-willed woman just to hang on through it all. You can read the entire account of Abraham and Sarah in the book of Genesis. For now, I would like to focus on a couple of specific instances.

Abraham and Sarah were blessed, but not because they did everything right. Sarah manipulated, used, and even abused others as she tried to force God's will and timing. Abraham lied, used his wife, and basically prostituted her to save himself. Was God there with her when Abraham failed to be the husband he should have been? If indeed women were objects to God, wouldn't He have expected her to just cope with the consequences of Abraham's actions? After all, that would have meant that only Abraham was the important one, and therefore, her feelings in the situation would have been of little importance. God's heart on the matter is clearly found in scripture. The events in the following passage took place before God changed the names of Abram and Sarai to Abraham and Sarah. It is no surprise that her name means "my princess."

Now there was a famine in the land, and Abram went down to Egypt to live there for a while because the famine was severe. As he was about to enter Egypt, he said to his wife Sarai, "I know what a beautiful woman you are. When the Egyptians see you, they will say, 'This is his wife.' Then they will kill me but will let you live. Say you are my sister, so that I will be treated well for your sake and my life will be spared because of you."

When Abram came to Egypt, the Egyptians saw that she was a very beautiful woman. And when Pharaoh's officials saw her, they praised her to Pharaoh, and she was taken into his palace. **He treated Abram well for her sake, and Abram acquired sheep and cattle, male and female donkeys, menservants and maidservants, and camels.**

But the Lord inflicted serious diseases on Pharaoh and his household **because of Abram's wife Sarai.** *So Pharaoh summoned Abram. "What have you done to me?" he said. "Why didn't you tell me she was your wife? Why did you say, 'She is my sister,' so that I took her to be my wife? Now then, here is your wife. Take her and go!" Then Pharaoh gave orders about Abram to his men, and they sent him on his way, with his wife and everything he had (Genesis 12:10–20 NIV, emphasis added).*

Was Sarai insignificant? Was she only an object to be used for her husband's profit and a pharaoh's pleasure? Absolutely not! Her husband acted cowardly and selfishly in every way. So why did the situation end so beautifully for him? He went to Egypt in need during a time of famine, yet he left with not only the wife he had irresponsibly and deceitfully used, but also sheep, cattle, donkeys, servants, and camels. He left Egypt in abundance even though he had lied and prostituted his wife. Clearly, it was not his actions that caused this blessing. Why? Why was Abram protected and provided for so graciously in the midst of his abominable failure? The answer is twofold:

I believe it was more than her beauty and his desire for Sarai that caused Pharaoh to show such goodwill toward Abram. The favor of God himself rested upon Sarai, and her husband was richly blessed because of it. This is evident again in Genesis 20 when they are in a similar situation. Notice that Pharaoh's household was inflicted with disease not because of Abram, but *because of his wife.* God was keenly aware of the circumstance in which she had been unjustly and most probably, reluctantly placed. Abram had failed miserably as a husband, but God himself was her Protector and Provider. He always saw her, and He was always working on her behalf.

Another reason for the blessing was that God had made a promise to Abram. God is always faithful to protect the integrity of His Word. His promise was not dependent upon Abraham's perfection or lack of it. Likewise, in your life, even in the midst of weakness, mistakes, and failures, if you have entered into covenant with Him by making Jesus your Lord, God will guard over you and His Word in your life. This is the beauty of the Gospel of Jesus Christ! You will never be perfect, yet because of Jesus and the blood He shed, you are a child of the Most High God! Abraham and Sarah are shining examples of God's faithfulness in spite of the weakness of humanity. He loves you, He sees you, and He is always working on your behalf.

> *And we know that in all things God works for the good of those who love Him, who have been called according to His purpose (Romans 8:28).*

SEEN BY GOD

Now consider Hagar, the Egyptian maidservant of Sarai. God had promised Abram that his descendants would be as numerous as the stars in the sky. Yet, in their old age, he and Sarai still had no child. Not surprisingly, Sarai became impatient with God's timing and took matters into her own hands. She even blamed God for her infertility. In reality, though, God's timing would be perfect. Yet Sarai was unwilling to wait on the Lord and everyone paid dearly for her recklessness. In desperation and haste for a child, she sent her husband in to sleep with her maidservant, Hagar.

> *So he went in to Hagar, and she conceived. And when she saw that she had conceived, her mistress became despised in her eyes.*

> *Then Sarai said to Abram, "My wrong be upon you! I gave my maid into your embrace; and when she saw that she had conceived, I became despised in her eyes. The Lord judge between you and me."*

> *So Abram said to Sarai, "Indeed your maid is in your hand; do to her as you please."*

And when Sarai dealt harshly with her, she fled from her presence.

Now an Angel of the Lord found her by a spring of water in the wilderness, by the spring on the way to Shur. And He said, "Hagar, Sarai's maid, where have you come from, and where are you going?"

She said, "I am fleeing from the presence of my mistress Sarai."

The Angel of the Lord said to her, "Return to your mistress, and submit yourself under her hand." Then the Angel of the Lord said to her, "I will multiply your descendants exceedingly, so that they shall not be counted for multitude." And the Angel of the Lord said to her:

"Behold, you are with child,

> *And you shall bear a son.*
> *You shall call his name Ishmael,*
> *Because the Lord has heard your affliction.*
> *He shall be a wild man;*
> *His hand shall be against every man,*
> *And every man's hand against him.*
> *And he shall dwell in the presence of all his brethren."*

Then she called the name of the Lord who spoke to her, You-Are-the-God-Who-Sees; for she said, "Have I also here seen Him who sees me?" (Genesis 16:4–13)

It is not difficult to sympathize with the impatience of Sarai. She was no longer a young woman, and bearing children didn't seem likely for her anymore. Having children, especially male children, was of extreme importance for women. If they were unable to produce, they were looked at differently from other women. It was perfectly acceptable and lawful for Sarai to use her maidservant as a surrogate mother according to the standards of the world. It was, however, not part of God's perfect plan. Technically the promise of God had only been voiced to Abram. Sarai was very likely wondering if His plan even included her at all. If she had pondered on the heart of God, however, she would have realized that as "flesh of his flesh," when God made a promise to Abram, He was making the same promise to her.

By taking matters into her own hands, Sarai opened herself and her household up to chaos. Once Hagar found out she was pregnant, she felt a sense of pride and purpose that caused her to despise and provoke Sarai. Jealousy, hatred, and all manner of strife ensued. Sarai became so enraged in it all that she began to mistreat Hagar who fled, clearly in agony.

The mistreatment must have been unbearable for this servant to leave her only means of survival. Abram and Sarai had probably obtained her during their time in Egypt. In all likelihood, Hagar was feeling unparalleled loneliness, unworthiness, grief, and fear for her future. What would come of an unwed, pregnant, runaway maidservant? Grave possibilities and unpleasant scenarios must have raced through her mind. Hot tears of hopelessness and despair surely streaked down her face as she fled, putting more and more distance between herself and her only known security in a foreign land.

In the eyes of the world and probably in her own eyes, Hagar appeared replaceable and of little worth. To God, however, she was of great significance. He pursued her and appeared to her in her darkest hour. As she sat by the spring grieving and seething, God Himself appeared to her and changed everything. As He conversed with her, she gained a newness of strength and purpose. He never reprimanded her; He only gave her promises and instructed her to return to Sarai. I'm not sure how much any of that even mattered to her, though. Just the fact that the Lord cared for her and that He actually saw her and appeared to her transformed her life from the inside. She fled her situation feeling used and insignificant, but she undoubtedly returned feeling like the very jewel of God Himself. While her difficult situation remained, she must have been radiating joy as she returned to the very circumstance that had brought her so much pain. She now had the hope, strength, and joy to cope, for she knew she was not alone.

Hagar's life exemplifies how God sees every detail of your life. He never leaves you alone, and His presence changes everything. To know that the God of the universe, the Great I Am, and the Giver of life itself actually *sees you* right where you are will transform your world.

When I realized that God had seen every tear, every detail, and every injustice, my life changed. I realized that I had never, ever been alone, even though God had also seen my every flaw and every sin. Still, He loved me and had compassion on me. The realization of His love and presence in my life gave me new strength, boldness, and the ability to walk through even the most difficult circumstances.

He sees you wherever you are, wherever you have been, and in spite of what you have done. Open your heart and receive unsurpassed strength from the God who sees you!

AN UNLIKELY HERO

Now, consider Rahab. She was a prostitute and seemed like a most unlikely candidate to receive anything from God. She lived in Jericho where Joshua had secretly sent two spies to investigate before entering the Promised Land at the Lord's command. She showed great fear of the Lord and for His favored people, and she put her reverence into action. She bravely risked her own life for that of the two spies from Israel and God exalted her for her trust in Him. As you read the passage about her, imagine that this is a woman who has no respect from man, yet she is honored by Yahweh.

Then Joshua son of Nun secretly sent two spies from Shittim. "Go, look over the land," he said, "especially Jericho." So they went and entered the house of a prostitute named Rahab and stayed there. The king of Jericho was told, "Look! Some of the Israelites have come here tonight to spy out the land." So the king of Jericho sent this message to Rahab: "Bring out the men who came to you and entered your house because they have come to spy out the whole land." But the woman had taken the two men and hidden them. She said, "Yes, the men came to me, but I did not know where they had come from. At dusk, when it was time to close the city gate, the men left. I don't know which way they went. Go after them." (But she had taken them up to the roof and hidden them under the stalks of flax she had laid out on the roof.) So the men set out in pursuit of the spies on the road that leads to the fords of the Jordan, and as soon as the pursuers had gone out, the gate was shut.

Before the spies lay down for the night, she went up on the roof and said to them, "I know that the Lord has given this land to you and that a great fear of you has fallen on us, so that all who live in this country are melting in fear because of you. We have heard how the Lord dried up the water of the Red Sea for you when you came out of Egypt, and what you did to Sihon and Og, the two kings of the Amorites east of the Jordan, whom you completely destroyed. When we heard of it, our hearts melted and everyone's courage failed because of you, for the Lord your God is God in heaven above and on the earth below. Now then, please swear to me by the Lord that you will show kindness to my family, because I have shown kindness to you. Give me a sure sign that you will spare the lives of my father and mother, my brothers and sisters, and all who belong to them, and that you will save us from death."

"Our lives for your lives!" the men assured her. "If you don't tell what we are doing, we will treat you

kindly and faithfully when the Lord gives us the land" (Joshua 2:1–14 NIV).

The spies did not end up at Rahab's door by some cosmic coincidence. They were there by Divine appointment. Rahab had been hand-chosen by God for this assignment. Although she was a woman of no importance in the eyes of the world, she had become enthralled with the thought of a God who parts seas and fights battles for His people. As she pondered the stories she heard, she must have hoped for such a God to exist. She longed for a God who would accept her and love her that much.

Somewhere along the way, Rahab's hope gave birth to faith. She professed her belief in and her reverence for the God of Heaven and Earth. She acted on her faith by saving the lives of two strangers whom she knew belonged to this wonderful, all-powerful God. This profession wasn't made at the altar of a church, but instead, in the inner depths of her heart. She believed and changed history because of it. Once a woman of ill repute with whom no person of any importance would associate, Rahab became part of the very lineage of Christ Himself! She is not only the second woman mentioned in the New Testament (Matthew 1), but she is also mentioned in James 2:25 and in Hebrews 11, the chapter of faith, with great ones such as Abraham, Sarah, Noah, and others.

Rahab was more than accepted; she was magnificently exalted by the God in whom she put her trust. Although she possessed limited knowledge about God at the time, she humbly and willingly risked her life for His plan. Oh, how the Lord wants to shower you with His blessings. Simply trust Him and allow your faith to burst forth and produce action.

As you look to the Biblical accounts of those who have gone before you, and as you hear testimonies of those whose lives have been forever changed by the saving, healing love of God, may you, like Rahab, allow hope to rise in your heart and give birth to faith that will forever change your destiny.

Sarah, Hagar, and Rahab are a few shining examples of the value God places on His daughters. After the fall of mankind in the Garden of Eden, women quickly became mere objects and possessions in society. It is shown throughout the scriptures. This perversion, however, was *never* God's intention for His daughters.

I clearly remember an instance when God whispered to me. In my turmoil and questioning, I asked the Lord if He placed more value on men than women. The Lord turned my question into an answer. In my heart, I heard the question, "Do you love your son any more or less than you love your daughters? Do you place higher value on your son that you do on your daughters?" Without hesitation, my answer was a resounding "No ... I love each of my children more than life and they are equally invaluable to me!" The Lord made it clear to me in that moment that His heart is that of a perfect, loving, Father, and we as His sons *and* daughters are His priceless treasures. May you also walk in the knowledge of that truth today!

JESUS SHOWED THE WAY

Now, turn your attention to Jesus Christ Himself, the long-awaited Messiah, God in the flesh, the One who changed everything because of His love for humanity. People talk about Jesus and tell the stories of His life, death, and resurrection with such complacency. In reality, however, it is impossible within the finite human mind to truly comprehend His glory, His beauty, or His worth. Christ came to set the captives free. According to 2 Corinthians 5:21, He did not just carry the sin of the world. Jesus actually *became* sin so you and I could become the righteousness of God. This is so much more than anything the human mind can fully fathom.

Jesus did nothing of His own accord, but only that which He saw His Father do (John 5:19). His purpose was to bring the Father's perfect will to earth. There-fore, when you see Jesus honoring women, healing the sick, or raising the dead, you can know with cer-tainty that this was all part of the Father's will. Since God never changes, and He is everlasting, you can also know that His will to do all the things that Jesus did still remains today. With Jesus now seated at the right hand of the Father until His glorious return, you are now charged with being His ambassador, seeing to it that His will is accomplished through your life on earth.

One of the great things that Jesus did was promote women and protect and stand for their rights. Jesus never once demeaned or disallowed women. In the following passages, you will see the lives of a few other unlikely candidates and how meeting Jesus changed everything for them.

John chapter 4 describes an instance of Jesus purposefully going through Samaria. As He sat near the well and rested, a woman approached. Known only as "the woman by the well," this unnamed person may be one of the most infamous women in all of the New Testament. Living an ordinary and no doubt empty life, she was going about her daily routine when she had an unexpected, divine encounter with Jesus. If you read the details of this account, you will find that it brings to light the myriad of prejudices prevalent during the time. The mere fact that she was a woman made her an unlikely candidate for an open, public conversation with a man, and especially a Jewish man.

Jesus asked the woman for a drink as she drew water from the well. The conversation turned to the woman and her life of sin. Jesus ministered to her and disclosed His identity to her. This is especially interesting since Jews and Samaritans did not associate with one another. Samaritans were a pagan, mixed-race people group and were considered by the Jews to be "unclean." According to this thought process and the Law, if Jesus drank from the container touched by the Samaritan, He would become ceremonially unclean. As ridiculous as it may seem, it is not so different from prejudices in the world today such as inhumane treatment of Jews, African Americans, and women. These have occurred in the not so distant past and are no less preposterous.

Isn't it beautiful that Jesus was not afraid to be alone with this woman? His actions broke every unspoken law of the time and culture in which He lived. Not only was she a Samaritan and a woman, but she was a woman living in adultery! She had no dignity, and she unquestionably lived under a heavy cloak of shame. Yet, it was to her that He first revealed His identity as the Messiah. He wasn't afraid of her, nor was He fretting over the possibility that she might make a false accusation against Him and ruin His ministry.

Sadly, in today's culture full of lawsuits and accusations, women are often treated with distrust. Most professions, including those involving ministry, have safeguards against being alone with a woman. While it is important to guard yourself, your family, and your ministry, never forget that *agape* love crosses every race, age, and gender. Of utmost importance is staying in tune with the Holy Spirit to know how *He* would have you minister. It is tragic that some ministers are so concerned with themselves and their own protection that they fail to obediently minister to people of the opposite sex in any situation.

I thank God for the pastor who mentored me and was unafraid to approach me or have me plop down in his office with fears, tears, and questions. If he had treated me with distrust and kept me at a "safe distance," I would not be where I am today. It was through this pastor that I was able to see my Heavenly Father's love for me: the very same love that brought healing to my broken soul. To this day, this man is a spiritual father to me, and has made an unspeakable difference in my life. I thank God that he, like Jesus, was more concerned with my transformation than he was about following every social rule.

Likewise, Jesus took a risk by interacting with this Samaritan woman, yet He was unconcerned about what everyone might think. Instead, He followed the will of His Father and ministered to her with truth and love. As a result, she became His first evangelist, passionately leading many to eternal life through Christ. What a magnificent revelation of the gracious God who meets you right where you are!

Jesus' trip to Samaria was no accident. John 4:4 reveals that "He needed to go through Samaria." Jesus knew exactly where He was going that day. Most Jews went out of their way to *avoid* Samaria because of the deep disdain they held for the people there. Jesus, however, went there with purpose, knowing it was time to reveal Himself to the world as their anticipated Savior. He also knew precisely the person He intended to use to get His message out. First, though, He saw the Samaritan woman's individual needs and met them with compassion. Through the time and love He invested in her, a complete race of people was introduced to the love of Christ.

John 4:39 goes on to say that "many of the Samaritans from that town believed in Him because of the woman's testimony." How ironic, that a woman of such poor reputation could influence a whole city to such a great degree. Notice she went to fill her jars at an odd time. She did not go at sunrise or sunset, but in the heat of the day. It is likely that she did this to avoid others who she knew viewed her as an immoral outcast. She came to the well in shame, hoping to be unnoticed. However, once Jesus spoke into her life, she left her water pot to go to the very people she was previously trying to avoid! Only an encounter with Jesus Himself could cause such boldness to rise up in this withdrawn Samaritan woman who had previously been paralyzed by shame. Her excitement and transformation was so evident that not only did people *not* shun her, but they actually listened to her and followed her to meet Jesus!

*And at this point His disciples came, and **they marveled that He talked with a woman**; yet no one said, "What do you seek?" or, "Why are You talking with her?"*

The woman then left her water pot, went her way into the city, and said to the men, "Come, see a Man who told me all things that I ever did. Could this be the Christ?" Then they went out of the city and came to Him (John 4:27–30, emphasis added).

God is so multifaceted. Jesus did not just travel to Samaria that day to minister to this lost woman and her people, but to set precedence for all of humanity. He wanted His disciples and the world to see His love for this woman. He desired for her and everyone present to know how the Father saw her. He confounded the minds of many that day to demonstrate how the love of God far surpasses any cultural or social rules that man can establish. To Almighty God, she was not a second choice, nor was she an inadequate person in any way. Instead, she was a treasured, divinely appointed messenger of God. He could have remained culturally correct and selected a man, but instead He chose her.

Surely many, including His own disciples, were left scratching their heads in that moment as they saw Jesus by example raise the standard on how women are to be treated. He knew they were watching as He planted new seeds—of honor, respect, and value that He intended to grow and change the world for His glory. Thank God for Jesus, Our Advocate!!

RADICAL WORSHIP

Are you familiar with Mary of Bethany? Perhaps one of the most beautiful accounts in all of the Bible of Jesus' heart toward women is found in the passage of scripture about her:

And being in Bethany at the house of Simon the leper, as He sat at the table, a woman came having an alabaster flask of very costly oil of spikenard. Then she broke the flask and poured it on His head. But there were some who were indignant among themselves, and said, "Why was this fragrant oil wasted: For it might have been sold for more than three hundred denarii and given to the poor." And they criticized her sharply.

But Jesus said, "Let her alone. Why do you trouble her? She has done a good work for Me. For you have the poor with you always, and whenever you wish you may do them good; but Me you do not have always. She has done what she could. She has come beforehand to anoint My body for burial. Assuredly, I say to you, wherever this gospel is preached in the whole world, what this woman has done will also be told as a memorial to her."

Then Judas Iscariot, one of the twelve, went to the chief priests to betray Him to them. And when they heard it, they were glad, and promised to give him money. So he sought how he might conveniently betray Him (Mark 14:3–11).

Although she remains nameless in this passage, Mary of Bethany poured out what may very well have been her most valuable earthly possession in an act of worship to her Lord. As she poured the perfume over the head of Jesus, onlookers were appalled. The word "indignant" is used in scripture to describe their strong reaction. The use of the word "indignant" indicates more than just an annoyance. It is a description of very strong feeling. These men were insulted and offended.

What might have caused this great displeasure? Perhaps it was simply that she was using such expensive perfume for anointing Jesus instead of using it to feed the poor. Maybe it was some other reason altogether. Were they angered that the woman honored Jesus? Was it offensive to them that Jesus allowed her to do such a thing? Is it possible that they were angered with the audacity of a woman to be so bold? Wasn't she simply to serve them? One can only guess all that was in the hearts and minds of the disciples that day, but the Word says that they became indignant and that they rebuked her harshly.

Notice that Jesus then turned and reprimanded *them*. He not only defended her and permitted her act of devotion, but he also *honored* her. He magnified her act of worship, calling it a "good thing" that would be remembered everywhere and for all time whenever the gospel was preached. He lovingly elevated this woman who was bold enough to push through the traditions of men to demonstrate her devotion and love toward Him.

In the day and culture in which she lived, women were not allowed to learn in the same way as men. They were not considered of enough worth to educate. They were to stay beneath men in every way. What do you think gave this woman the courage to enter this room full of men and take center stage? Was it her willingness to be seen or some desire to make a statement? I think it was something much, much deeper.

She had come to humbly worship Jesus from the depths of her being. She must have known that she would cause a scene by taking such a valuable asset and pouring it out in front of an entire room full of people. Yet, something in her was greater than her fear. It burned within in her bosom despite the logic and law that told her she had no rights to do what she did or to disrupt the gathering in such a way. Her love, passion, and adoration for Jesus drove her to do the unacceptable. Somewhere along the way He had become the Lover of her soul, and she was willing to pay any price to express her full surrender to Him.

Mark 14:10 indicates that this elevation of a woman by Jesus may have been the proverbial straw that broke the camel's back for Judas Iscariot. Seeds had undoubtedly already been planted in his heart and mind, but it seems that this act of Jesus honoring Mary of Bethany was more than he could take. He immediately went to the chief priests to sell out the One whom he had once called his Lord.

You see, for generations, men had become exalted while women were devalued and debased. By correcting these men for rebuking her, Jesus was sending a message straight from the heart of God. It was a message of the worth of this woman and all women. Judas Iscariot, already full of pride, was less than willing to agree. Instead, he chose a path that would allow him to cling to his rigid beliefs and fill his pockets with gold.

IN SEARCH OF TRUTH

You have just studied a few of the many profound scriptures dedicated to revealing the tender, loving heart God has toward His daughters. Perhaps something you have read here has shed light on some incorrect beliefs that you have always held true. Let the revelation of the heart of God sink into your soul and answer questions that lie deep within.

The Church has a responsibility to seek truth, even when it means changing mindsets that have been in place for many generations. Half of the Body of Christ has been taken out by toxic lies that have poisoned the minds of both men and women. If only women will realize who they are in Christ and stop living lives of passivity, and men will lay down their pride and stand up for what the Bible *truly* says about women. God desires that you be empowered and fueled with the truth that sets yourself and others free. He desires for the Body of Christ to bring His Kingdom to earth in perfect peace and unity, with the strength that can only come by walking hand in hand *together* as sons and daughters of our gracious Father.

chapter 3

GOD'S HEART FOR HIS SONS

For He foreordained us (destined us, planned in love for us) to be adopted (revealed) as His own children through Jesus Christ, in accordance with the purpose of His will [because it pleased Him and was His kind intent] ~ Ephesians 1:5 (AMP)

YOU ARE SIGNIFICANT

Women are not the only ones who have been targeted by the Father of Lies. Many men are also plagued by vicious lies and self-doubt. The enemy sets special traps for men to convince them that they must prove themselves to themselves, others, and God. The truth, however, is that God loves you deeply without any expectation of performance. He accepts you, and He longs for you to see yourself through His eyes of truth.

It is not up to your wife, children, parents, boss, co-workers, employees, or anyone else to impart your value to you. Your worth is not determined by the size of your bank account or the professional accomplishments you may or may not have attained in this life. Instead, your sense of significance and purpose should come from God alone. Go directly to the heart of your Father God and ask Him to show you your worth and significance as defined by Him. You are a winner and a success in His eyes, and He wants you to open yourself up to *His* truth.

A man does not have to be of great physical stature to be important in the eyes of God. It is a lie from the enemy to believe that you must be a certain size or physical strength to be a real man. Look at the life of a little man by the name of Zacchaeus in the following passage of scripture:

And [Jesus] entered Jericho and was passing through it.

And there was a man called Zacchaeus, a chief tax collector, and [he was] rich.

And he was trying to see Jesus, which One He was, but he could not on account of the crowd, because he was small in stature.

So he ran on ahead and climbed up in a sycamore tree in order to see Him, for He was about to pass that way.

And when Jesus reached the place, He looked up and said to him, Zacchaeus, hurry and come down; for I must stay at your house today.

So he hurried and came down, and he received and welcomed Him joyfully.

And when the people saw it, they all muttered among themselves and indignantly complained, He has gone in to be the guest of and lodge with a man who is devoted to sin and preeminently a sinner.

So then Zacchaeus stood up and solemnly declared to the Lord, See, Lord, the half of my goods I [now] give [by way of restoration] to the poor, and if I have cheated anyone out of anything, I [now] restore four times as much.

And Jesus said to him, Today is [Messianic and spiritual] salvation come to [all the members of] this household, since Zacchaeus too is a [real spiritual] son of Abraham;

For the Son of Man came to seek and to save that which was lost (Luke 19:1–10 AMP).

Small stature did not keep Zacchaeus from being a man in the eyes of Jesus. Zacchaeus was probably less than confident in himself. Although he seemed to be a wealthy man, he had attained his riches by taking advantage of others. He had to go to bed with that on his conscience every night. His riches did not make him feel like a man. They did not satisfy his soul, so he went in search of Jesus. He couldn't have looked like much of a macho man as he climbed a tree in hopes of just getting a glimpse of the One who could give his life true meaning and worth.

Because he was a tax collector, he had little respect from those around him. In fact, the people around Jesus complained because He was going to eat with this man who they considered to be a sinner. Jesus defied all of their theology by going to the home of Zacchaeus anyway. While He was there, He declared salvation and great significance over the house of this man who was small in the eyes of the world but valued greatly by his Father God.

Surely from that moment forward, the life of Zacchaeus took on new meaning. He had been called a son of Abraham by Jesus. He had gone from being a little man in a tree searching for answers to a man of worth in the eyes of the Savior of the world. His life was most likely completely transformed as the familiar lies of insignificance were swept away in the rushing water of the words of love and acceptance he heard that day.

Words of insignificance in your life do not come from your Father God. They are seeds thrown out by the enemy of your soul and they are looking for a place to take root. Refuse to take them into the garden of your heart. You are a son of Abraham, and God is completely for you. As you invite him to join you at the table of your soul, He will speak forth words of acceptance and truth. Listen to Him today, and be forever changed.

Turning to the Old Testament book of Judges, you can read about a man named Gideon. The Israelites had disobeyed God and refused to listen to Him time and time again. The result was oppression and destruction, just the opposite of all God desired to give them. Gideon was going about life under the heavy weight of oppression when he found himself face to face with the Lord.

> *Now the Angel of the Lord came and sat under the terebinth tree which was in Ophrah, which belonged to Joash the Abiezrite, while his son Gideon threshed wheat in the winepress, in order to hide it from the Midianites. **And the Angel of the Lord appeared to him, and said to him, "The Lord is with you, you mighty man of valor!"***
>
> *Gideon said to Him, "O my lord, if the Lord is with us, why then has all this happened to us? And where are all His miracles which our fathers told us about, saying, 'Did not the Lord bring us up from Egypt?' But now the Lord has forsaken us and delivered us into the hands of the Midianites."*
>
> *Then the Lord turned to him and said, "Go in this might of yours, and you shall save Israel from the hand of the Midianites. Have I not sent you?"*
>
> *So he said to Him, "O my Lord, how can I save Israel? Indeed my clan is the weakest in Manasseh, and I am the least in my father's house."*
>
> *And the Lord said to him, "Surely I will be with you, and you shall defeat the Midianites as one man." (Judges 6:11–16, emphasis added)*

Gideon was not looking for any accolades or war hero titles when the Angel of the Lord approached him. He was doing what may have seemed like a menial job, just trying to get by and protect what he could from the Midianites. At that point in Gideon's life, he likely saw himself as less than significant. He was living in what appeared to be "survival mode" and most likely did not feel like much of an accomplished man. However, God saw Gideon through a completely different set of eyes, and He had a mission for him to fulfill.

The Angel of the Lord referred to Gideon as a "mighty man of valor" even though Gideon clearly did not see it. He referred to himself as the "least" in his father's house, and described his clan as the "weakest in Manasseh." His confidence in himself as a man and warrior was small. Still, God had chosen him and saw him as His brave and mighty son.

Gideon's faith in God seemed almost as weak as his confidence in his own ability. If you continue reading through Judges 6, you will find that Gideon was hesitant to believe he was speaking with the Lord. He sought a sign from Him. Once Gideon got beyond his insecurity and believed the words that God spoke of him, he went into battle and defeated the Midianites. He chose to listen to the truth of God about who he was. He was not a man without significance. He was valiant and chosen in the sight of God.

The Lord declares significance over your life. Perhaps you are a man of strong and mighty stature or a man with great education and phenomenal career accomplishments. On the other hand, maybe you are a man of little worth according to the standards of this world. Your life may be marked by financial or personal failure. You are not defined by your temporary accomplishments or failures of this world. Regardless of where you find yourself today, you are His mighty son. You were created in His image, and therefore, you were created with strength and purpose. You need not rely on the respect or opinion of others to shape your opinion of yourself. Look solely to your Father for words of acceptance and identity.

Do not compare yourself to others and attempt to measure up according to who they might be. Your strength is unique to your calling, and you are able to accomplish the things He has called *you* by name to achieve. Trust His word over your life. He calls you a "son of Abraham" and His "mighty son of valor!" See yourself through His eyes of pure truth and dare to step out into the realm of faith as He calls you forth for His purposes and for His glory.

NO LONGER FATHERLESS

This world is full of broken families and broken hearts. Far too many sons and daughters are without earthly fathers to show them the way. In many homes, the father may be present physically, but missing emotionally. Perhaps he is harsh and authoritative instead of patient and loving. The godly role of a father in the life of his child is of utmost importance. If you are one of those sons who grew up without an earthly father or with a father who did not meet your needs, your Heavenly Father is ready and willing to show you the way.

Whether you were raised with no father, a harsh father, or even an abusive father, your perfect Heavenly Father calls you by name. He sees you where you are, and He knows where you have been. Even if your earthly father missed it, your Heavenly Father *never* missed one of your ball games or other important moments of your life. Whether you were aware or not, He was with you and cheering you on every step of the way. Do not allow the enemy to define you and direct your life based on the failures of your earthly father. That void can be filled to overflowing with the goodness and abundant love of your Father God. As the Holy Spirit guides you into all truth, you can see through spiritual eyes and recognize the wounds that may have been inflicted through your pain. Let God be your Daddy and your Healer as you run to Him with childlike faith to fill the empty space in your heart.

It is common to put up fronts to guard your heart from pain. This usually ends up hurting those who love you the most as those safeguards keep everyone away, even those you love. Let the walls of protection that you have built around yourself fall to the ground as you sit in the presence of the Holy One. Only He can make all things new and make you into the man that He intended for you to be. He can only accomplish these wondrous things in your life if you allow Him to. He waits patiently for you to turn to His loving arms and seek Him for wholeness and restoration.

PRIDE AND EMOTIONS

Men tend to be more reluctant than women to seek emotional healing. Society and wrong teaching have created men who believe they are not "real" men if they show emotion or ask for help. This all stems from pride. Brokenness is not only an issue among women. It is very real in the lives of men everywhere, and should be addressed by the Body of Christ in order to see individuals, marriages, and families healed.

While a woman may be more likely to discuss her turmoil and pain, a man is more likely to pretend there is no problem at all. Ignoring an issue will not make it better. If you have a gaping wound in your body and cover it up with an article of clothing, it does not mean that the wound has healed. Although it is temporarily out of sight, it is still there. It has just been covered up. To keep the wound from becoming infected or scarring, it must be properly treated. Likewise, ignoring an emotional wound or covering it up with something to keep it hidden does not make it go away. Left unattended, emotional wounds begin to ooze and infect those around you. Unfortunately, the people most often affected are those closest to you. An honest look within your heart is critical. The *only* way to healing is through the Healer.

Emotions are very much a part of who God created both men and women to be. Men were designed to show emotion. Jesus Himself showed great emotion during His earthly life. It was genuine compassion that moved Him toward people. He wept, He got angry, and He agonized. He allowed His heart to be touched with the weakness of humanity, and it caused Him to move and act in faith. He healed, touched, restored, and made whole those who were in need. His emotion was not a weakness; it was a conduit for the power and love of God to flow through.

A MAN AFTER THE HEART OF GOD

David was known as "a man after God's own heart." I would imagine that most Christian men would like to be referred to in such a great way. What made David worthy of this title? There were many reasons why David might have been described in such a way. None of them are because of his pride or lack of emotion. Nor are they a result of his perfection. David was passionate about His God, and he was not afraid to let it show.

Then David danced before the LORD with all his might; and David was wearing a linen ephod. So David and all the house of Israel brought up the ark of the LORD with shouting and with the sound of the trumpet.

Now as the ark of the LORD came into the City of David, Michal, Saul's daughter, looked through a window and saw King David leaping and whirling before the LORD; and she despised him in her heart. So they brought the ark of the LORD, and set it in its place in the midst of the tabernacle that David had erected for it. Then David offered burnt offerings and peace offerings before the LORD. And when David had finished offering burnt offerings and peace offerings, he blessed the people in the name of the LORD of hosts. Then he distributed among all the people, among the whole multitude of Israel, both the women and the men, to everyone a loaf of bread, a piece of meat, and a cake of raisins. So all the people departed, everyone to his house.

Then David returned to bless his household. And Michal the daughter of Saul came out to meet David, and said, "How glorious was the king of Israel today, uncovering himself today in the eyes of the maids of his servants, as one of the base fellows shamelessly uncovers himself!"

*So David said to Michal, "It was before the L*ORD*, who chose me instead of your father and all his house, to appoint me ruler over the people of the L*ORD*, over Israel. Therefore* **I will play music before the LORD. And I will be even more undignified than this,** *and will be humble in my own sight. But as for the maidservants of whom you have spoken, by them I will be held in honor." (2 Samuel 6:14–21, emphasis added)*

This passage vividly depicts something that is a dilemma in the lives of many Christian men. It is a commonplace belief that a show of emotion signifies weakness, while remaining unmoved is a sign of strength. This thought process is rooted in pride and self-centeredness. David was looked down upon by his wife for his radical show of emotion. In her eyes, he did not appear "manly" or haughty enough. David refused to let pride stop him, though, as he vowed to be even more radical in his worship to God. The enemy used David's wife to attempt to discredit him as a man, but David knew the truth and remained unmoved.

The Psalms of David also show the great emotion that he experienced as he cried out to God at various times. David was a powerful king, a successful warrior, and an attractive man according to descriptions of him throughout scripture. He could have easily become consumed with his conquests and prideful of his masculine image, yet he remained humble before God. You can read many accounts about him in the Old Testament, and you will find that he was a worshipper to his core. He was not afraid to lay everything aside, including his favor with man and his influential position in the world, to worship God. It did not matter to him what anyone thought. He adored God and expressed it passionately.

You have already discovered that David had his share of failure. His perfection was not what qualified him to be described by God as one after His own heart. When David sinned and fell short, however, he was always willing to repent before the Lord. Psalm 51 reveals that his repentance was just as marked by passion as his worship. He cried out to God for forgiveness. David did not live in the New Covenant of Grace that you and I live in today. His prayer found in Psalm 51 is a wonderful picture of the heart of David and the man that he was, but this is not the same prayer that a born again believer living in the New Covenant would pray. The point, however, is that David understood the gracious heart of God enough to come before him and repent. He loved God wholeheartedly and knew he could go to Him in time of need or failure. He drew his strength and identity from God alone.

A man after the heart of God will not be afraid to show emotion, worship God, and repent when necessary. God took great pleasure in seeing these things in the life of David. He takes great pleasure in you, His son, when He sees them in your life as well. Ask Him to show you how to let your guard down and worship Him as if no one else matters. Let Him gently teach you how to sit before Him and relinquish control of your emotions to Him. Every negative thing and every wrong word spoken over you will melt away in His presence. You are His, and He will faithfully show you the way to His heart.

THE LIE OF DOMINATION

One of the greatest perversions in the universe is the lie Satan tells men in regards to domination. Men were created with a desire to conquer, overcome, and lead. This is wonderful until it crosses over into the realm of domination through manipulation, intimidation, or other ungodly ways. Leadership and dominance are not synonymous. They are completely opposite of each other. As you can see from the following passage, the issue of male dominance was part of the curse:

And the Lord God said to the serpent, Because you have done this, you are cursed above all [domestic] animals and above every [wild] living thing of the field; upon your belly you shall go, and you shall eat dust [and what it contains] all the days of your life.

And I will put enmity between you and the woman, and between your offspring and her Offspring; He will bruise and tread your head underfoot, and you will lie in wait and bruise His heel.

*To the woman He said, I will greatly multiply your grief and your suffering in pregnancy and the pangs of childbearing; with spasms of distress you will bring forth children. Yet **your desire and craving will be for your husband, and he will rule over you.***

And to Adam He said, Because you have listened and given heed to the voice of your wife and have eaten of the tree of which I commanded you, saying, You shall not eat of it, the ground is under a curse because of you; in sorrow and toil shall you eat [of the fruits] of it all the days of your life.

Thorns also and thistles shall it bring forth for you, and you shall eat the plants of the field.

In the sweat of your face shall you eat bread until you return to the ground, for out of it you were taken; for dust you are and to dust you shall return (Genesis 3:14–19 AMP, emphasis added).

This passage outlines the details of the curse of sin. It is the moment in time when God gave a thorough account to Adam, Eve, and Satan of the consequence of their disobedience. As God speaks to Eve, he mentions that her husband will rule over her. When God originally created Adam and Eve, it was His intention for them to be co-rulers over the earth and everything in it. As you can see from the following account, they were *never* designed to rule over each other.

*Then God said, "Let Us make man in Our image, according to Our likeness; **let them have dominion over the fish of the sea, over the birds of the air, and over the cattle, over all the earth and over every creeping thing that creeps on the earth." So** God created man in His own image; in the image of God He created him; **male and female** He created them. Then God blessed them, and God said to **them**, "Be fruitful and multiply; fill the earth and **subdue it; have dominion over the fish of the sea, over the birds of the air, and over every living thing that moves on the earth"** (Genesis 1:26–28, emphasis added).*

Both husband and wife were made in the image of God and possessed the boldness and ability within them to rule over and subdue the earth. The desire to lead was purposefully placed within *both* of them, yet there was no strife. At no time did God instruct man and woman to rule, subdue, or have dominion over one another. The curse, however, described a very different scenario. Eve would no longer partner peacefully with Adam. Instead, he would "rule over her." This created chaos within men and women as individuals as well as within the marriage relationship. God had created marriage with perfect purpose, but through sin Satan was able to enter in and come between the participants of that beautiful and divinely created relationship.

Instead of unity and peace, there was competition and strife. The God-given authority they once shared became an ever-present point of contention. In the eyes of man, woman was no longer considered a co-ruler. The ability God had put in man to lead and rule over the earth became a distorted need to control, and it no longer only applied to fish of the sea, birds of the air, and animals that roamed the earth. Now, it also applied to his wife and others in his life.

This is a lie that is planted in the hearts of men from an early age. It has been passed from generation to generation. Some men try to control everyone around them through intimidation, anger, oppression, or other ungodly methods. These are *not* qualities indicative of leadership or Biblical headship. Instead, it is the fruit of fear and insecurity, and it is a gross misrepresentation of what God originally intended. True headship is rooted in love and is all about giving, serving, protecting, and encouraging. Dominance, on the other hand, oppresses, selfishly demands, puts others down, and seeks to control. This type of tyranny is a trap from Satan sent to ruin individuals, marriages, and families. Sadly, however, it is encouraged and taught even in many Christian homes and churches.

REDEEMED FROM THE CURSE

Christ redeemed us from that self-defeating, cursed life by absorbing it completely into himself. Do you remember the Scripture that says, "Cursed is everyone who hangs on a tree"? That is what happened when Jesus was nailed to the cross: He became a curse, and at the same time dissolved the curse ... (Galatians 3:13–15 MSG)

The wonderful news is that mankind has been redeemed from the curse. There is no longer a need to be bound by the doom and oppression of it. To refuse freedom from any area of the curse is to say that Jesus became your sacrifice in vain. Jesus came to show the better way. With the help and revelation of the Spirit of God within, you *can* lead like Jesus without being dominant, forceful, harsh, and controlling. That was never God's way in the first place.

Men are not alone in this battle. There are women who try to dominate their husbands. This, too, is a fruit of fear and insecurity. The contention and struggle for power within a marriage should not be. It has been nailed to the cross, and both partners are free to love and honor each other, creating an environment of peace, unity, and fruitfulness. That is the heart of God.

Take a candid look at your life and how you deal with others. Do you talk down to other people? Do you treat your wife as if you are the boss? Do you use intimidation to lead your home and your children? Do you expect others to honor and respect you without you ever having to earn it or show respect to them? Do you believe that your home is designed by God as a tyrannical hierarchy with you being the most important? Are you demanding and heavy-handed with others? These are a few questions that may help you discover poisonous roots of the destructive lie of domination in your life.

If you find that you have succumbed to the deception of the enemy in this area, simply go to the throne of grace. Draw on the endless mercy of your Father God. He is for you, and He is more than able to help you overcome. Begin to meditate on how God loves you and how Jesus led in His earthly ministry. As you grasp His true nature of love and grace, you will be able to uproot the seeds that have taken root in your life. These seeds grow into weeds and choke the life out of your relationships with others. As you draw on His grace and strength, you will find the relationships in your life flourishing that were once stale and cold. Your marriage will become a place of peace, joy, and pleasure. You will see your children run to you as you are able to run to your Heavenly Father. People in your life will begin to honor and respect you not because you demand it from them, but because they are drawn to the love and light within you. With a humble heart and the help of the Holy Spirit, you can change.

BREAKING FREE

Men are a picture of the strength, wisdom, and protection of God. As a man, you possess qualities unique to the sons of God. He desires that you see yourself the way He sees you. Like Zacchaeus, you are completely accepted by Him. Like Gideon, you are mighty and valiant in His eyes. Like David, you can run to His arms and give yourself fully to Him without fear of rejection.

Forget negative words that may have been spoken over you in the past, or things you have been incorrectly taught. He longs for you to hear His voice today, and to push all other voices aside. Let the walls of stone crumble to the ground as you rest in Him and submit to Him. Allow your identity as a man, husband, father, son, and friend come from Him alone. He will empower you to the degree that you submit yourself to Him. You are His dearly beloved son, and He is proud of you!

chapter 4

THE FORCE OF FORGIVENESS

Keep your heart with all diligence,
For out of it spring the issues of life. ~ Proverbs
4:23

THE CHOICE BELONGS TO YOU

You have looked at the love of your Heavenly Father in a earlier chapters and seen His willingness and heart's desire to bless you abundantly. However, there are things that can hinder the abundant life He has provided. Failing to forgive and holding on to bitterness do *not* change God's love toward you, but they can quickly inhibit the flow of God's blessings in your life. Much like a clogged artery, unforgiveness impedes the life-giving blood and spiritual oxygen to your heart and makes you less sensitive to the things of God.

As is the case with many of the lies of the enemy, sometimes you may not realize that you are holding resentment toward a person. Other times it may be glaring, with the hurt or offense constantly on your mind. It may be gnawing away at you constantly, or it may be something in the distant past that you have failed to deal with along the way. In any case, *any* root of bitterness in the life of a believer must be dealt with in order to walk fully in the joy and abundance of the Lord.

There are so many things in the Christian walk that are simply your choice. Oftentimes, these are things you simply cannot accomplish in your own strength, yet they depend on your decision. Forgiveness is one of those choices. You cannot control the actions of others, or things that may be said about you or done to you, but you *can* guard your heart with all diligence. Jesus said that offenses *would* come (Matthew 18:7). It isn't a question of if they will come; it is inevitable. Yet, you choose whether or not you will let those offenses enter your heart.

Whether you have been abandoned, abused in any way, rejected, slandered, or even left for dead, you *can* forgive the one who hurt you. Holding offense and unforgiveness in your heart does nothing to correct the behavior of another. It also does not cause the person to be remorseful or pay for what they have done. Instead, it hardens the heart of the one who is choosing to not forgive. Forgiveness is not about who is right and who is wrong. It is all about you keeping your heart soft and open to the things of God. Why would you want something in your heart that would keep you from experiencing all that God has for you?

LET GOD BE GOD

You may have been wounded during a time of wandering. Maybe it was a consequence of your own bad choices or the choices of someone with whom you allowed a place of influence in your life. On the other hand, perhaps you were living a wonderful life, serving God, when a brother, sister, or minister in the Body of Christ hurt you deeply and unexpectedly. These wounds can be especially hurtful as expectations are set high for ministers and fellow believers. Always remember, though, that not everyone who comes in the name of the Lord accurately represents the heart of the Lord.

You may have been treated badly by a family member or betrayed by a close friend or even your spouse. You may have been rejected by a parent or someone you loved deeply with whom you desired to have a meaningful relationship. Regardless of where the pain came from, it was never planned for you by your Heavenly Father. Now, no matter how deep the wound, He wants you to give it to Him instead of carrying it on your own. He puts it beautifully in the following verse:

Come to Me, all you who labor and are heavy-laden and overburdened, and I will cause you to rest. [I will ease and relieve and refresh your souls.] Take My yoke upon you and learn of Me, for I am gentle (meek) and humble (lowly) in heart, and you will find rest (relief and ease and refreshment and recreation and blessed quiet) for your souls (Matthew 11:28, AMP).

Holding on to offense and bitterness is anything but restful. On the contrary, it causes many other issues including unrest, depression, and even physical disease. To refuse to lay any offense or situation at the feet of Jesus is to fail to trust in Him. It is an attempt to be God. When you refuse to forgive and let go of offense, you are exalting yourself above God Almighty in your own heart and mind. The results can be devastating. His yoke is easy and light, not heavy and oppressive. The choice is yours.

One of the greatest examples in scripture regarding forgiveness is found in Genesis 37—50. Joseph was born to Jacob and Rachel and was set apart for the purposes of God. He walked in great favor with his father, but his brothers resented him. When God revealed His plans to Joseph in a dream, Joseph excitedly shared this dream with his brothers. Instead of being happy for him, jealousy raged within his brothers. They sold him into slavery and convinced their father that he had been killed. They resented the favor that Joseph walked in, and they despised him because of his boldness to think that they would ever bow to him as his dream indicated.

When Joseph had come to his brothers, they stripped him of his [distinctive] long garment which he was wearing;

Then they took him and cast him into the [well-like] pit which was empty; there was no water in it.

Then they sat down to eat their lunch. When they looked up, behold, they saw a caravan of Ishmaelites [mixed Arabians] coming from Gilead, with their camels bearing gum [of the styrax tree], balm

*(balsam), and myrrh or ladanum, going on their
way to carry them down to Egypt.*

*And Judah said to his brothers, What do we gain if
we slay our brother and conceal his blood?*

*Come, let us sell him to the Ishmaelites [and
Midianites, these mixed Arabians who are
approaching], and let not our hand be upon him,
for he is our brother and our flesh. And his brothers
consented.*

*Then as the Midianite [and Ishmaelite] merchants
were passing by, the brothers pulled Joseph up and
lifted him out of the well. And they sold him for
twenty pieces of silver to the Ishmaelites, who took
Joseph [captive] into Egypt (Genesis 37:23–28,
AMP).*

The years that followed for Joseph included much
heartache, including being falsely accused by Potipher's
wife and being imprisoned even though he was an
innocent man. Joseph unquestionably had much
opportunity for discouragement and resentment to
build in his heart and mind. As he sat in a cold, dusty
prison cell, he must have been tempted with thoughts
of hatred and resentment toward his brothers who
had betrayed him and left him for dead. People he
trusted with the dreams of his heart had rejected and
despised him. These were people he loved immensely.
His wounds were deep, and his anger could have been
easily justified.

Joseph made a choice, however, to keep his heart free from hatred and open to the heart of God. He refused to let a root of bitterness grow in his life, even as he walked through the many dark and lonely years. It would have been so easy during that difficult time to turn away from all he had believed about God. Instead, he focused on the faithfulness of God and the plans that had been promised him in his dreams. Throughout his life and in each situation, Joseph showed great character, never seeming as a man without hope or importance.

Joseph had continuous favor throughout his life, regardless of the circumstances that surrounded him. He valued his relationship with God above all else, even though at times it appeared God had forgotten him. He chose truth and honor instead of caving to the lies and temptation that sought to entangle him. He never allowed himself to be bound by sin, resentment, or unforgiveness. As a result of Joseph's efforts to guard his heart and live a life of forgiveness in the midst of unthinkable circumstances, he was elevated and honored, eventually becoming one of the most powerful leaders in the kingdom.

After he was released from prison and promoted to a position of authority in Egypt, Joseph's brothers unknowingly entered his life once again. These were the very same brothers who betrayed him, left him for dead, and lied to his father about him. Again, Joseph made a choice. In his position of power he could have easily taken revenge into his own hands and made them suffer for all they had done. At the very least, he could have used his power and authority to intimidate them and make them grovel in their pain. He could have sought justification by his own hands. Instead, he humbly and lovingly vowed to care for them and encouraged them to forgive themselves as he revealed his identity to them in a deeply emotional moment for all of them.

Then Joseph said to his brothers, "I am Joseph; does my father still live?" But his brothers could not answer him, for they were dismayed in his presence. And Joseph said to his brothers, "Please come near to me." So they came near. Then he said: "I am Joseph your brother, whom you sold into Egypt. But now, **do not therefore be grieved or angry with yourselves because you sold me here**; *for God sent me before you to preserve life. For these two years the famine has been in the land, and there are still five years in which there will be neither plowing nor harvesting. And God sent me before you to preserve a posterity for you in the earth, and to save your lives by a great deliverance. So now it was not you who sent me here, but God; and He has made me a father to Pharaoh, and lord of all his house, and a ruler throughout all the land of Egypt.*

"Hurry and go up to my father, and say to him, 'Thus says your son Joseph: "God has made me lord of all Egypt; come down to me, do not tarry. You shall dwell in the land of Goshen, and you shall be near to me, you and your children, your children's children, your flocks and your herds, and all that you have. There I will provide for you, lest you and

your household, and all that you have, come to poverty; for there are still five years of famine."

"And behold, your eyes and the eyes of my brother Benjamin see that it is my mouth that speaks to you. So you shall tell my father of all my glory in Egypt, and of all that you have seen; and you shall hurry and bring my father down here." **Then he fell on his brother Benjamin's neck and wept, and Benjamin wept on his neck. Moreover he kissed all his brothers and wept over them, and after that his brothers talked with him** *(Genesis 45:3– 15, emphasis added).*

Even after all the horrific things his brothers had plotted and done to him, Joseph still loved them deeply. Their acts of selfishness had changed the course of his life, yet he forgave them. Had he allowed his heart to become hard with bitterness, he would not have been able to show this genuine expression of love for them. He hugged them, wept over them, and kissed them. It is evident by the emotion he expressed that he had endured great pain. It is possible to forgive even in the midst of deep emotional hurt. Although the hurt may remain for some time, the choice to forgive is an open door for the healing touch of God to enter your soul.

Joseph exemplified how important it is to forgive others, and the blessings that flow from choosing to forgive as opposed to carrying a burden of resentment. If Joseph had held hatred and bitterness toward his brothers who had left him for dead and discarded him as if he had no value, he would have missed out on the plans God had for his life. He would have missed out on the promotion God had planned for him, and he would have failed to become the prominent ruler of Egypt. If he had been focused on how to get even, he would not have had the opportunity to bless his brothers richly. Most importantly, if he had focused on all the hurt instead of his relationship with God, he would have failed to become the great man and leader God had created him to be.

THE ISSUE OF TRUST

Regardless of how deeply someone in your life has hurt you, or how long you have carried the burden in your heart, God stands with his hands open, ready to take it from you. Remember, this is a spiritual decision. Be aware that your emotions may not follow along right away. It also does not mean you will or should trust the person you are forgiving. For example, I have forgiven the person who sexually abused me, but I would never leave my children in his care. Although Joseph most probably forgave Potipher's wife for falsely accusing him, I doubt he ever spent time alone with her again after his release from prison.

Forgiveness does not automatically equate to trust. Choosing forgiveness does not mean you must put yourself in the hands of the person who hurt you. It is not wrong to forgive from a distance and sometimes that is how it must be. At other times, it is appropriate to go to the person and talk things out. It really depends on the circumstance and the leading of the Holy Spirit within you. Again, remember that forgiveness has nothing to do with who is right or wrong, or the willingness of the other person to repent. Forgiveness is about *your* heart and your walk with God. It is about setting yourself free from bondage to another person and from the shackles of bitterness.

You do not forgive from your emotions; you forgive from your spirit. You may truly choose to forgive a person and yet continue to have the same feelings of disdain or anger rise up within you. It takes time for your emotions to catch up with your decision to forgive. Take authority over your thoughts and remind your emotions that you have forgiven that person by choice. Then focus on the goodness of God in your life, realizing you have chosen life by choosing forgiveness.

You may be in a situation that requires you to forgive repeatedly. Perhaps your boss mistreats you often or a co-worker lies about you on a regular basis. You may be in a marriage where your spouse insults you or takes you for granted daily. In these instances, purpose to lean minute by minute on the Holy Spirit and walk out a lifestyle of forgiveness. You cannot do it in your own strength, but the power of Christ in you will enable you to do it. You have received abundant forgiveness through Christ, and because He lives in you, you can freely extend it to others.

FORGIVING YOU

Another aspect of forgiveness that is often overlooked is forgiveness of self. Because of lies of self-condemnation, guilt, and shame, you may be able to forgive everyone in your life, yet you may still hold yourself hostage by failing to forgive yourself. This happened in my own life. I had several symptoms of unforgiveness including anger and depression. As I searched my heart and asked the Holy Spirit to reveal to me whom it was I had not forgiven, I came up blank. I had purposed in my heart to forgive every person who had hurt me throughout my life. As I went through faces and names of people beginning in my early childhood, I could think of no one that I had failed to forgive. As I stood in the presence of the Lord that day, he gently spoke to me that it was *me* whom I had not forgiven.

The realization that I had not forgiven myself came as a shock to me. I began to realize that I had not counted myself worthy of forgiveness. The Holy Spirit spoke to me that it was no less wrong for me to fail to forgive myself than it was to hold hatred toward other people. In fact, He told me it was pride. I was failing to do for myself what Jesus had already done for me. In walking in what I thought to be humility, I was actually succumbing to pride. That day I laid my self-hatred at the feet of Jesus and began a process of learning to love myself and humble myself before Him.

This is a common problem among believers. Perhaps you have had an abortion, shattered your family with adultery or divorce, mistreated someone, or even committed crimes. God wants you to forgive yourself. To believe that your sin is too big for the blood of Jesus to cover is pride.

Failing to forgive self is especially common among women and their partners who have chosen abortion. Oftentimes it is after they go on to have children later in life, or find that they are unable to bear children after abortion that they begin to carry a heavy load of guilt and condemnation, feeling unworthy of the forgiveness of Christ. This could not be further from truth. Jesus did *not* endure the cross in vain. Neither did He only die for what we as humans consider "lesser sins." He died for *all* your sin, including abortion, fornication, adultery, and any other horrific thing you may have done.

Your sin, no matter how unthinkable, is no different from the little white lie you told when you were a child to keep yourself out of trouble. Satan loves nothing more than for you to consider your sin as being unforgivable. This keeps you at a distance from God, believing the lie that you cannot be loved as much as Saint Suzie who never openly sinned in her life and was even a virgin on her wedding day. You are no less righteous in the sight of God than Brother Bob who has always followed God, loved his family, and never even cussed. These things are wonderful, and there is no doubt that Suzie and Bob have been blessed as a result of their faithfulness. Just like the Prodigal Son, however, you are placed right alongside Sister Suzie and Brother Bob in perfect standing with God the minute you say "Yes!" to Jesus and all He did for you. God does not put you at the back of the line. He removes your sin as far as the east is from the west and you become what He has always had planned for you: holy, pure, and righteous in His sight! If He can forgive and forget it, you should, too!

Looking back once again to the account of Joseph and his brothers, you can see how difficult it can be to forgive yourself:

When Joseph's brothers saw that their father was dead, they said, "Perhaps Joseph will hate us, and may actually repay us for all the evil which we did to him." So they sent messengers to Joseph, saying, "Before your father died he commanded, saying, 'Thus you shall say to Joseph: "I beg you, please forgive the trespass of your brothers and their sin; for they did evil to you."' Now, please, forgive the trespass of the servants of the God of your father." And Joseph wept when they spoke to him.

Then his brothers also went and fell down before his face, and they said, "Behold, we are your servants."

Joseph said to them, "Do not be afraid, for am I in the place of God? But as for you, you meant evil against me; but God meant it for good, in order to bring it about as it is this day, to save many people alive. Now therefore, do not be afraid; I will provide for you and your little ones." And he comforted them and spoke kindly to them (Genesis 50:15–21).

Even after Joseph had proclaimed his love and forgiveness for his brothers, and encouraged them not to be angry with themselves, they could not free themselves from their trespasses. They lived with guilt and condemnation for many years. In their minds, what they had done to him was deserving of punishment. Again, Joseph was grieved by their lack of trust and willingness to forgive themselves. Still, he gently reassured them that he had forgiven them and encouraged them to do the same. He even pointed out that he was not in the place of God to judge them. Likewise, do not exalt yourself to a seat of judgment over your life and the lives of others. Forgive yourself, forgive others, and let God be God in every circumstance.

STAND YOUR GROUND

Even after you choose to forget it and move on with your life, you will likely be reminded of your past by the enemy. Oftentimes, he will use people to bring it up to you, by asking questions or making comments that make you feel as though you have been punched in the stomach. Just as you have finally put the past in the past and the wound is beginning to heal, someone comes along and rips it open with thoughtless words. This has happened to me more times than I can count. It hurts deeply, and it is not from God. Many times these people have no idea how they are being used by the enemy. Forgive them for their ignorance, and stand in who you are, knowing you are dearly loved and perfectly forgiven. I have often said that nosiness is *not* a fruit of the Spirit and has no place in the Body of Christ. Just because you have a brother or sister who has fallen into this trap does not mean you are not forgiven. Let it go, and do not pick up the condemnation or shame that Satan attempts to replant in your heart.

The force of forgiveness is powerful. It opens the door of your heart to the things of God, it opens your life to the bountiful flow of blessings He desires for you, and it makes you usable in His kingdom in mighty ways. Forgive others, forgive yourself, and let your past be forever forgotten. Turn the tides on the enemy of your soul and use forgiveness and your testimony to overcome his schemes in your life and relationships. You will be amazed at the results as you release yourself from the prison of bitterness, hatred, and resentment, and walk into the abundant life of joy that He designed for you!

chapter 5

WORTHY, NOT WORTHLESS

For as he thinks in his heart, so is he ... ~
Proverbs 23:7

TAKE A CLOSER LOOK

Satan loves to cause you to think you are of no value to this world or to God. Thoughts of unworthiness plague millions of men, women, and children. These thoughts usually begin at a very early age. Your enemy strives for you to believe you are nothing, especially to God. He wants you to feel less valuable than others around you who may appear more "together" or more "holy." When you accept that lie, you lose your sense of purpose and hope. Instead of feeling capable of overcoming any and every obstacle in your life, you begin to feel defeated and incapable. Many times these thoughts keep you from doing anything in the Kingdom of God at all, even though the call God has placed on your life is enormous.

Thoughts you think about yourself matter. They determine your future. What you meditate on becomes who you are. It becomes the decisions you make in life. Your thought life literally has the power to determine your destiny.

The Israelites are a perfect example of the power of thoughts. The Lord had promised them the Land of Canaan, a land full of abundance. When the Lord spoke to Moses and told him to send men to spy out the land, he never mentioned that going into the land was optional. Moses chose twelve men, including Joshua and Caleb to go search out the land and bring back a report. The spies found wonderful things in the land. They found abundant fruit including a huge cluster of grapes they cut down and took back with them.

Now they departed and came back to Moses and Aaron and all the congregation of the children of Israel in the Wilderness of Paran, at Kadesh; they brought back word to them and to all the congregation, and showed them the fruit of the land. Then they told him, and said: "We went to the land where you sent us. It truly flows with milk and honey, and this is its fruit. Nevertheless the people who dwell in the land are strong; the cities are fortified and very large; moreover we saw the descendants of Anak there. The Amalekites dwell in the land of the South; the Hittites, the Jebusites, and the Amorites dwell in the mountains; and the Canaanites dwell by the sea and along the banks of the Jordan."

Then Caleb quieted the people before Moses, and said, "Let us go up at once and take possession, for we are well able to overcome it."

But the men who had gone up with him said, "We are not able to go up against the people, for they are stronger than we." And they gave the children of Israel a bad report of the land which they had spied out, saying, "The land through which we have gone as spies is a land that devours its inhabitants, and all the people whom we saw in it are men of great stature. There we saw the giants (the descendants of Anak came from the giants); and we were like grasshoppers in our own sight, and so we were in their sight" (Numbers 13:26–33, emphasis added).

God gave the spies plenty to be hopeful about. I doubt it was coincidence that He chose to send them during the season of ripe grapes. It took two men to carry one cluster! It was only a couple of chapters earlier in the book of Numbers that the Israelites were complaining about God's menu choices for them. This bountiful fruit represented the abundant life God was so eager to give them.

So what happened? Why would they not recognize the favor and blessing upon their lives and simply walk in it? The reason became clear as the men who were with Joshua and Caleb described the thoughts that they had chosen to believe. In their minds, they believed they looked like grasshoppers and their adversaries looked to be giants. Caleb and Joshua, however, described something entirely different. They chose to look through a different lens. They peered through a lens of hope and truth, knowing God was with them. They described the land in a completely different way in the following passage:

> *But Joshua the son of Nun and Caleb the son of Jephunneh, who were among those who had spied out the land, tore their clothes; and they spoke to all the congregation of the children of Israel, saying: "The land we passed through to spy out is an exceedingly good land. If the Lord delights in us, then He will bring us into this land and give it to us, 'a land which flows with milk and honey'"* (Numbers 14:6–8).

Caleb and Joshua knew they could do it. They knew they had the favor of God, and that with Him they could take the land. They were not dependent on their own abilities, but on their position and good standing with God. It was His word and His promise that made all the difference to them.

On the contrary, the other spies were simply looking in the natural realm. They considered their own abilities and lack of stature. They meditated and focused on doubt and negativity. This resulted in a huge sacrifice for everyone. Instead of entering the land of abundance God had promised them, they lived out the remainder of their lives in the wilderness. Only Joshua and Caleb, who went against the popular opinion and chose to see through the eyes of God, were allowed to enter the land of plenty that God had intended for them all.

HOW DO YOU SEE YOURSELF?

It is easy to see yourself and your situation in the natural realm. It is not difficult to focus on your imperfections, shortcomings, and lack of talent. Your enemy goes to great lengths to plant these seeds of self-doubt through negative thoughts and various situations from your earliest years. I have seen and heard children say some of the most hurtful things to one another, not realizing they are being used by the enemy. Parents oftentimes carelessly speak words that cause seeds of rejection to take root in the heart of their children. Words are powerful and they are meant to be spoken with purpose.

It is common to live with regret, shame, guilt, and condemnation when you have made mistakes or been wounded or used by others. None of these will lead to a victorious, productive life. In fact, it is these very thoughts that can eventually lead people to suicide. They meditate on their worthlessness for so long that they finally accept thoughts of suicide as normal, believing that the world around them is better off without them in it. They continue to think on their lack of value until they eventually do the unthinkable.

Regardless of what anyone has told you, the lies you may have believed your whole life, or the things you may have done, the truth is that you are treasured by your Father God. You have not been rejected, abandoned, or condemned. On the contrary, you have been accepted, purposed, and dearly loved. In fact, God loved you so much that He sent His only Son to become the perfect sacrifice so you could be placed in righteous standing with Him, inheriting abundant, eternal life.

You are in a much more wonderful position than Joshua and Caleb were in. They did not have the New Covenant of Grace. Jesus had not yet come to this earth. Jesus did not come as a temporary solution. He *became* sin, so you could become righteous! Religion makes Him a temporary solution, requiring you to get born again over and over after every mistake. Because of what Jesus did for you, you are now a joint heir with Him! How much more worthy can you possibly get? You only need to believe that it is true!

HIS WORTH, NOT YOURS

Not that we are fit (qualified and sufficient in ability) of ourselves to form personal judgments or to claim or count anything as coming from us, but our power and ability and sufficiency are from God.

[It is He] Who has qualified us [making us to be fit and worthy and sufficient] as ministers and dispensers of a new covenant [of salvation through Christ]... (2 Corinthians 3:5–6 AMP).

This world is full of influences telling you the value of self-confidence, self-gratification, self-promotion, and self-happiness. True worth, however, is none of those things. You are nothing in and of yourself. Regardless of how educated, accomplished, or talented you may be, you are incapable and undeserving apart from Christ. Perhaps you were born again at an early age and have never missed church or lived in overt sin.

Even so, your own righteousness means nothing. The Amplified Bible says it like this:

> *For we have all become like one who is unclean [ceremonially, like a leper], and all our righteousness (our best deeds of rightness and justice) is like filthy rags or a polluted garment; we all fade like a leaf, and our iniquities, like the wind, take us away [far from God's favor, hurrying us toward destruction] (Isaiah 64:6, AMP).*

It is trust in the blood of Jesus alone that makes you worthy, and it makes you worthy indeed! Once you accept His gift of righteousness, you are as holy, blameless, and perfect in the sight of God as Jesus is. To fail to accept and believe it is to declare that what Jesus did for you is not sufficient. What Jesus did is plenty big enough to cover anything and everything you may or may not have done in your life. Stop looking at yourself, your abilities, or your failures. You are worthy because He has made you worthy!

I once lived under a very heavy cloud of condemnation. No matter how much I loved God, I never felt worthy enough to receive His love, forgiveness, or any other gift He had provided for me. I can remember people telling me to meditate and speak, "I am the righteousness of God in Christ Jesus." The problem was that I felt so unworthy that I could not even comprehend the meaning of what I was saying. It took me many, many months of meditating on truth to reach a point of even beginning to understand the meaning of those words. It was only after I began to get revelation in that area that I began to walk with new hope, purpose, and confidence.

Focusing on self in any way, shape, or form is pride. While unworthiness may seem like low self-esteem and even humility, it is really just the opposite. You will accomplish very little in the kingdom of God by focusing on *you*. When you are begging, pleading, and wallowing in your insecurities, you are not doing much good for anyone else. This is why it is *false* humility. The enemy wants you to believe you are humble as he keeps you in this non-productive mindset. True humility focuses on God and His ability in and through you. It does not deny Him power in your life.

When you begin to focus and meditate on who you are because of Christ, and all that you can accomplish with Him in you, then you become a powerhouse in the Kingdom of God, and a vessel of true humility. He wants you to discover the purpose that He has for you. He wants you to know how powerfully He can move through you. He desires for you to walk in boldness and confidence in every area of your life, not because of who *you* are, but because of who *He* is in you!

Seeing then that we have a great High Priest who has passed through the heavens, Jesus the Son of God, let us hold fast our confession. For we do not have a High Priest who cannot sympathize with our weaknesses, but was in all points tempted as we are, yet without sin. Let us therefore come boldly to the throne of grace, that we may obtain mercy and find grace to help in time of need (Hebrews 4:16).

Because of Jesus, you are able to approach the throne of God in total confidence. You do not need to crawl to the altar praying you won't be struck down because of your unworthiness. Why would you spend your life begging and living in an unholy fear of God, believing you are of no worth, when He has made a way and has a desire for you to come boldly to Him? There is no sin too big, no problem too hard, no inadequacy too great to surpass the love, grace, and total sufficiency of Christ!

LET GO OF REGRET

Many times the reason for feelings of unworthiness stem from past sins and regrets. I hope you have discovered the importance of forgiving yourself. Even after you have forgiven yourself, however, you may find yourself mulling over regret in your mind. You may still feel unworthy to be used by God. Religion and traditions of men reinforce this lie. Some denominations will not allow you to minister if you have ever been divorced. You may feel called and yet feel it is too late because of mistakes and sins of your past. This is a lie you must reject so you can fully become the person God has created you to be, and to live the life He has planned for you.

The Apostle Peter gives great insight into overcoming failure. Peter loved Jesus immensely. He stepped out of the boat to go to Jesus on the water as the others sat in fear. He passionately followed Jesus during His time on earth. He vowed to die with Jesus if necessary. Yet, when the disciples abandoned Jesus in the Garden of Gethsemane, Peter was among them. Then, while Jesus faced the Sanhedrin, as Peter sat outside awaiting word about His Lord, he denied that he ever even knew Him.

Peter failed epically. Yet, he loved Jesus so much. How could he be such a coward? He let a moment of fear control him. He had told Jesus he was willing to die with Him. Instead, he acted as lowly as those who sought to take Jesus' life. Earlier, Jesus had shared with Peter and the others that if anyone denied Jesus before men, they would also be denied before their Heavenly Father. (Matthew 10:33) As Peter wept bitterly, I'm sure he remembered these words of Jesus. The enemy had used Peter, and he knew it. Could he even be forgiven? I'm sure he pondered thoughts such as these over and over in his mind in the days that followed this sad event.

Even after this abhorrent failure on Peter's part, however, he rose to the occasion in the book of Acts. After the death, burial, resurrection, and ascension of Jesus, Peter was in a different place. You have already seen the importance of forgiving yourself. Peter forgave himself. He was no longer groveling in condemnation, guilt, and shame for his sin. Peter's focus had shifted to Jesus as his Source, Strength, and Sufficiency. Acts 1:15 indicates that it was Peter who took control of the meeting to appoint a new disciple. Peter also boldly imparted healing as he made a lame man walk. Then, when the day of Pentecost came, and the crowd was baffled, Peter again stood and delivered a powerful message of redemption, which led 3,000 people to faith in Jesus Christ! Read the powerful accounts of Peter in the following passages:

But Peter, standing up with the eleven, raised his voice and said to them, "Men of Judea and all who dwell in Jerusalem, let this be known to you, and heed my words" (Acts 14:42).

Then Peter said to them, "Repent, and let every one of you be baptized in the name of Jesus Christ for the remission of sins; and you shall receive the gift of the Holy Spirit. For the promise is to you and to your children, and to all who are afar off, as many as the Lord our God will call."

And with many other words he testified and exhorted them, saying, "Be saved from this perverse generation." Then those who gladly received his word were baptized; and that day about three thousand souls were added to them (Acts 2:38–41).

And a certain man lame from his mother's womb was carried, whom they laid daily at the gate of the temple which is called Beautiful, to ask alms from those who entered the temple; who, seeing Peter and John about to go into the temple, asked for alms. And fixing his eyes on him, with John, Peter said, "Look at us." So he gave them his attention, expecting to receive something from them. Then Peter said, "Silver and gold I do not have, but what I do have I give you: In the name of Jesus Christ of Nazareth, rise up and walk." And he took him by the right hand and lifted him up, and immediately his feet and ankle bones received strength. (Acts 3:2–7)

Without question, Peter experienced guilt for his denial of Jesus. Just like you, Peter was unquestionably inundated with lies of his unworthiness because of his actions. Peter, however, chose truth. He ran to Jesus for His forgiveness. He fully believed in the redemptive work of the Cross. Had he chosen to focus on the lies of unworthiness, he would have completely missed out on the mighty foundational work of the Church Age that God had destined for him. Had he looked to himself and all his imperfections in the natural, he never would have been able to stand and take charge of the meetings. He never would have been able to allow the message of the Gospel to flow out of him. Had he looked to His own ability and holiness, it would have been impossible for him to take the lame man at the gate by the hand and see him walk. He chose to cast down the lies of the enemy and thoughts of unworthiness and instead become a vessel for Jesus to live through. What a difference his decision made for all of us!

Judas could have made the same choice. His betrayal of Jesus was no greater sin than Peter's. God's heart toward Judas was just as tender as His heart toward Peter. Judas chose death; God did not choose it for him. If Judas, like Peter, had looked to Jesus and accepted forgiveness, he could have gone on to live an abundant life just like Peter went on to experience. Even though he betrayed Jesus unto death, he could have reached out and drawn on the Grace of God and lived. Instead, he focused on his sin, shame, and guilt, and it cost him his own life.

When morning came, all the chief priests and elders of the people plotted against Jesus to put Him to death. And when they had bound Him, they led Him away and delivered Him to Pontius Pilate the governor.

Then Judas, His betrayer, seeing that He had been condemned, was remorseful and brought back the thirty pieces of silver to the chief priests and elders, saying, "I have sinned by betraying innocent blood."

And they said, "What is that to us? You see to it!"

Then he threw down the pieces of silver in the temple and departed, and went and hanged himself (Matthew 27:1–5).

This sad ending to the life of Judas could have been avoided. He simply could not carry the burden of guilt for all he had done. It seems deserving for him, though, right? After all, he had betrayed Jesus. As difficult as it is to comprehend, Judas had the same opportunity as Peter. It would be easy to say, "Oh Judas had hardened his heart. He was reprobate." These scriptures indicate differently. He felt horrible for his actions and tried to undo the situation in his own strength before it was too late. He wanted to go back and change what he had done. Instead of turning to God's open arms of forgiveness, though, he focused on the guilt of his actions until he completely lost hope and took his own life.

DARE TO BELIEVE

You have a choice every minute of every day. While the enemy bombards you with thoughts of your worthlessness, God waits and Jesus intercedes for you, praying that you will be strong in your faith and believe truth. What has God put in your heart? Who does He say you are? There are plans that God has for you that are beyond your wildest dreams. Today, may you choose to awaken those dreams as you walk with your head held high and your past far behind you, realizing that you take each and every step in the boldness and worth of Christ Jesus. Without Him, you are not able, but because of Him you are unstoppable!

chapter 6

FREEDOM FROM FEAR

There is no fear in love; but perfect love casts out fear, because fear involves torment. But he who fears has not been made perfect in love. ~ 1 John 4:18

FACING FEAR

Fear is by far one of the most effectual tools in the arsenal of our enemy. It comes cloaked in various ways, but its ultimate purpose is always the same: to render ineffective. It can cause a myriad of issues, from doubt, to nervousness, to serious physical problems including panic attacks and heart issues. It has a variety of labels and forms including intimidation, insecurity, worry, and anxiety. Jealousy is another form it takes. Jealousy is nothing short of fear. It ruins relationships, marriages, families, and individual lives. Regardless of the mask it wears, fear has kept an alarming number of people in the Body of Christ from becoming effective ministers of the gospel. Every single lie of the enemy is ultimately intertwined with fear. It is the rotten fruit of a bad root.

Fear became an extremely formidable part of my life from a very early age. Regardless of age, gender, intellect, social or economic status, fear has a way of creeping into various areas of life. In my case, it came through trauma and abuse, but it can come in different forms through different doors, far too many to mention in a single chapter of a book. Perhaps it entered your life through rejection or betrayal. Maybe it was through verbal or physical abuse you suffered. Often fear enters from simply meditating for too long on the cares, evil, and brokenness of this world. In any case, it needs to be addressed head on.

There are literally hundreds of scriptures in the Bible that talk about fear. That does not include those that use fear to describe reverence. A healthy fear of the Lord is reverence for Him, and it is in no way related to the terror or torment being addressed in this chapter. God does not want you to experience fear. It is debilitating and destructive. He wants you to rest and trust in Him, and that simply isn't possible when you are tormented by fear.

It was only a few short years ago when the Lord began to show me that fear had a tight grip in every area of my life. I was afraid of people, failure, death, and pretty much everything in between. While I am not here to tell you that this battle will necessarily be won for you in one easy step, I can help you see through the Word of God why it is worth the effort to recognize fear and learn to guard yourself against it. As you do, you will begin moving in the right direction: away from fear and into the realm of faith.

FEAR THAT CAUSED FAILURE

The Bible is packed full of examples for you. Most of them can be looked at from different angles and have many meaningful points. Oftentimes, though, when you learn a certain application for a particular story in the Bible, you never look at it from any other point of view. As you open your heart, receive fresh manna and new revelation from some familiar stories in the Bible.

Sometimes when you look at scripture and see great men and women of God, you can fail to see that these wonderful people were very much human. They dealt with all the same emotions as well as personal and relational issues that people deal with today. Do not shortchange yourself by only looking at the strengths of these great ones without considering all that they may have battled.

As you already know, Abraham himself, known as the father of our faith, dealt with fear. One of the lies of the enemy is the lie of isolation, which convinces you that no one else has dealt with what you are facing. You will see clearly from the following examples that even the greatest warriors in the Word battled the same fears you face today, and some let it overcome them.

David was a mighty man of God who is remembered for his greatness and his faith. More than once in scripture, though, you can see clues to the fear that he battled. One such moment is found in the book of 2 Samuel. David succumbs to temptation and commits adultery with Bathsheba. She was married to Uriah the Hittite who was a loyal commander in King David's army. While Uriah was away, Bathsheba became pregnant with David's child. As the following scriptures reveal, David's sin opened his life up to fear.

Then David sent to Joab, saying, "Send me Uriah the Hittite." And Joab sent Uriah to David. When Uriah had come to him, David asked how Joab was doing, and how the people were doing, and how the war prospered. And David said to Uriah, "Go down to your house and wash your feet." So Uriah departed from the king's house and a gift of food from the king followed him. But Uriah slept at the door of the king's house with all the servants of his lord, and did not go down to his house. So when they told David, saying, "Uriah did not go down to his house," David said to Uriah, "Did you not come from a journey? Why did you not go down to your house?"

And Uriah said to David, "The ark and Israel and Judah are dwelling in tents, and my lord Joab and the servants of my lord are encamped in the open fields. Shall I then go to my house to eat and drink, and to lie with my wife: As you live, and as your soul lives, I will not do this thing."

Then David said to Uriah, "Wait here today also, and tomorrow I will let you depart." So Uriah remained in Jerusalem that day and the next. Now when David called him, he ate and drank before him; and he made him drunk. And at evening he went out to lie on his bed with the servants of his lord, but he did not go down to his house.

In the morning it happened that David wrote a letter to Joab and sent it by the hand of Uriah. And he wrote in the letter, saying, "Set Uriah in the forefront of the hottest battle, and retreat from him, that he may be struck down and die." So it was, while Joab besieged the city, that he assigned Uriah to a place where he knew there were valiant men. Then the men of the city came out and fought with Joab. And some of the people of the servants of David fell; and Uriah the Hittite died also (2 Samuel 11:6–17).

Only a few short scriptures prior to this account, David seems to be virtually void of fear as he goes about conquering armies by faith in the Living God. Yet, he seems utterly consumed with it in these verses. His fear first pushed him to attempt to deceive Uriah into believing the baby Bathsheba carried was his own. Yet, when his attempts to hide his sin by deception failed, his fear drove him to murder an innocent man! While this may be an extreme example, it is important to realize that fear can cause you to do strange things. This snowball effect is not uncommon when you are dealing with fear and lies of the enemy.

Another example of fear at work is in the life of a man named Barak. This is a man of the Old Testament who had the potential to go down in the Bible as a great hero, yet he didn't. Does his name ring a bell?

It probably doesn't, because he allowed fear to determine his destiny.

> *Now Deborah, a prophetess, the wife of Lapidoth, was judging Israel at the time. And she would sit under the tree of Deborah between Ramah and Bethel in the mountains of Ephraim. And the children of Israel came up to her for judgment. Then she sent and called for Barak the son of Abinoam from Kedesh in Naphtali, and said to him, "Has not the Lord God of Israel commanded, 'Go and deploy troops at mount Tabor; take with you ten thousand men of the sons of Naphtali and of the sons of Zebulun; and against you I will deploy Sisera, the commander of Jabin's army, with his chariots and his multitude at the River Kishon; and I will deliver him into your hand'?"*
>
> *And Barak said to her, "If you will go with me, then I will go; but if you will not go with me, I will not go!"*
>
> *So she said, "I will surely go with you; nevertheless there will be no glory for you in the journey you are taking, for the Lord will sell Sisera into the hand of a woman." Then Deborah arose and went with Barak to Kedesh. And Barak called Zebulum and Naphtali to Kedesh; he went up with ten thousand men under his command, and Deborah went up with him (Judges 4:4–10).*

Scripture goes on to reveal that Barak did indeed conquer the army of Sisera. But you already knew that would happen, right? God Himself had already declared it would come to pass. He said with assurance that He would deliver this army into the hand of Israel. Barak was obviously a man of great courage and influence as he was in charge of ten thousand men. This should have been easy for him, especially since God had guaranteed victory. Yet, he needed to hold Deborah's hand for this battle. He allowed fear to rob him of great victory. Now, we all know the name of Deborah, but very few remember Barak. As Deborah stated, he gave up any recognition or influence he might have had all because of fear.

Perhaps this was a larger battle than Barak had ever been involved in, and he feared he was incapable. Is it possible that you have been chosen by God to do a great thing, and yet the fear of your own shortcomings holds you back? Barak had more confidence in Deborah than in himself. Yet, God had called Deborah to be Judge over Israel, not Commander of the army. He had chosen Barak to do that.

Likewise, it is not uncommon to see someone who is operating in great influence and fruitfulness in a particular area to be incorrectly assumed as having some special powers for every area of life and ministry. When you compare yourself to others, the result is usually either discouragement or pride. Neither is fruitful. When you feel less equipped or less favored by God for the task to which you have been called, you talk yourself out of it and miss out on great things that God has for you.

As you have already seen in a previous chapter, Peter faltered. He brilliantly demonstrated how the fear of man can cause one to act completely out of character. It was never his intention to betray Jesus. He loved Jesus passionately. He adamantly exclaimed his willingness to die with Jesus just hours before he denied him three separate times. Yet, fear gripped him in a moment of weakness and he vehemently denied the One he held so dear.

Now Peter sat outside in the courtyard. And a servant girl came to him, saying, "You also were with Jesus of Galilee."

But he denied it before them all, saying, "I do not know what you are saying."

And when he had gone out to the gateway, another girl saw him and said to those who were there, "This fellow also was with Jesus of Nazareth."

But again he denied with an oath, "I do not know the man!"

And a little later those who stood by came up and said to Peter, "Surely you also are one of them, for your speech betrays you."

Then he began to curse and swear, saying, "I do not know the Man!"

Immediately a rooster crowed. And Peter remembered the word of Jesus who had said to him, "Before the rooster crows, you will deny Me three times." So he went out and wept bitterly (Matthew 26:69–75).

Although it is not the case, it seems almost as if Peter was overtaken by some sort of spell. He denied Jesus just as ardently as he had exclaimed his willingness to die with him. This demonstrates how influential the fear of man can be. Have you ever said or done something and wondered where it even came from? It all originates with fear. The intent of Peter's heart was never to deny Jesus, yet he did because of a root of fear that dwelt there.

The world around you is full of very diverse ways of thinking. Many deny Jesus and ridicule those who call Him Lord. In those times, it can become almost automatic to suppress your true beliefs. Whether you call it peer pressure, intimidation, or some other name, it is fear. These fears will continue to control you until you recognize them and take your God-given authority over them.

THE COURAGE TO OVERCOME

There is much to learn regarding the subject of fear from those who have gone before you. God did not stop loving those you have read about who gave way to fear. He forgave and lovingly led them anyway. Yet, they missed out on blessings as a result of making fear their lord, if even for a moment. You have looked at a few of the many Biblical accounts of those who have allowed fear to influence their lives and steal from them. Now we will flip the proverbial coin and look at some examples of those who refused to allow fear to get in their way.

Now in the fourth watch of the night Jesus went to them, walking on the sea. And when the disciples saw Him walking on the sea, they were troubled, saying, "It is a ghost!" And they cried out for fear.

But immediately Jesus spoke to them, saying, "Be of good cheer! It is I; do not be afraid."

And Peter answered Him and said, "Lord, if it is You, command me to come to You on the water."

So He said, "Come." And when Peter had come down out of the boat, he walked on the water to go to Jesus. But when he saw that the wind was boisterous, he was afraid; and beginning to sink he cried out, saying, "Lord, save me!"

And immediately Jesus stretched out His hand and caught him, and said to him, "O you of little faith, why did you doubt?" And when they got into the boat, the wind ceased.

Then those who were in the boat came and worshiped Him, saying, "Truly You are the Son of God" (Matthew 14:25–33).

This story is commonly used to point out Peter's lack of faith. However, the most striking fact in this account is that Peter had to fight fear to even get out of the boat. He was the only one of all the folks in the boat who actually overcame fear and stepped out on the water with Jesus. Although it was short lived, Peter literally walked on water. Other than Jesus, Peter is the only person who has done it. He moved past his fear of the known to attempt the supernatural. Oh, what amazing things God has planned for you to experience if you are willing to just step out of the boat instead of staying nestled inside, gripped with fear of what could happen, all the while thinking you are keeping yourself safe!

Now, turn to the Old Testament and back to the mighty King David. David's sin led him to a place of fear and failure in a previous discussion. However, at other times he demonstrated amazing courage and willingness to overcome fear. He led numerous conquests of armies. He allowed Saul to live, even though Saul actively pursued David with the intent of taking his life. Now, take a closer look at an account you have probably heard for many years: David killed Goliath.

David, the youngest of eight sons was only a young boy when this event took place. He was responsible for caring for his father's sheep and running errands. When his father told him to take some things to his brothers who were on the battlefield in the army of Israel, he willingly obeyed. Upon his arrival, however, David found the giant Philistine, Goliath, antagonizing the army of Israel and causing them to flee in terror.

Then David spoke to the men who stood by him saying, "What shall be done for the man who kills this Philistine and takes away the reproach from Israel? For who is this uncircumcised Philistine, that he should defy the armies of the living God?" (1 Samuel 17:26)

This was a bold approach for such a young man with no experience in battle. It was not, however, egotistical in any way. You already know David as a "man after God's own heart." This verse beautifully reflects the passionate heart within him, even though he was very young. It indicates a righteous indignation that was rising up within him, giving him the boldness to not only overlook the insolent remarks and ridicule that followed, but to go on to face a hate-filled giant in battle.

Now when the words which David spoke were heard, they reported them to Saul; and he sent for him. Then David said to Saul, "Let no man's heart fail because of him; your servant will go and fight with this Philistine."

And Saul said to David, "You are not able to go against this Philistine to fight with him; for you are a youth, and he a man of war from his youth."

But David said to Saul, "Your servant used to keep his father's sheep, and when a lion or a bear came and took a lamb out of the flock, I went out after it and struck it, and delivered the lamb from its mouth; and when it arose against me, I caught it by its beard, and struck and killed it. Your servant has killed both lion and bear; and this uncircumcised Philistine will be like one of them, seeing he has defied the armies of the living God." Moreover David said, "The Lord, who delivered me from the paw of the lion and from the paw of the bear, He will deliver me from the hand of this Philistine."

And Saul said to David, "Go, and the lord be with you!" (1 Samuel 17:31–37)

These words of David depict anything but fear. He was filled with faith and confidence, and it caused Saul to show favor to him. He was not qualified to go into this fight by the standards of the Israeli army, his brothers, or the king. He was, however, confident in who he was and what he was called to do. He was certain that His God was alive, able, and willing to deliver him. He was qualified by God and God alone. He went on to even step out of the protective armor that the king supplied for him. In a world of degrees, certifications, and worldly requirements for aptitude, may you replace your fears of inadequacy with the revelation knowledge that your Maker has made you able. He unfailingly qualifies and equips you for that which He calls you to do.

Then he took his staff in his hand; and he chose for himself five smooth stones from the brook, and put them in a shepherd's bag, in a pouch which he had, and his sling was in his hand. And he drew near to the Philistine. So the Philistine came, and began drawing near to David, and the man who bore the shield went before him. And when the Philistine looked about and saw David, he disdained him; for he was only a youth, ruddy and good-looking. So the Philistine said to David, "Am I a dog, that you come to me with sticks?" And the Philistine cursed David by his gods. And the Philistine said to David, "Come to me, and I will give your flesh to the birds of the air and the beasts of the field!"

Then David said to the Philistine, "You come to me with a sword, with a spear, and with a javelin. But

*I come to you in the name of the Lord of hosts, the
God of the armies of Israel, whom you have defied.
This day the Lord will deliver your head from you.
And this day I will give the carcasses of the camp of
the Philistines to the birds of the air and the wild
beasts of the earth, that all the earth may know that
there is a God in Israel. Then all this assembly shall
know that the Lord does not save with sword and
spear; for the battle is the Lord's, and He will give
you into our hands" (1 Samuel 17:40–47).*

Of course, David did indeed slay the giant, with only
a slingshot and stone. This is both miraculous and
courageous. Think of the fear and lies David had to
overcome as he walked through this event. If he had
believed the lie that he was too young and inexperienced,
he would have never said a word to begin with. Yet, he
pushed through that lie and opened his mouth in an act
of faith, giving God something to work with.

He could have caved in to the fear of those around
him who hurled insults and hurtful accusations of in-
competence. Instead, he stood his ground. Notice that
while he was standing against the insults and lies, God
was working. Verse 29 tells us that David's words were
heard and reported to King Saul. God opened a door
for David as a direct result of his willingness to act in
faith, instead of staying silent or running in fear.

Beyond all of that, however, David still had to face
the giant himself. That was enough to cause him to
shake in terror if nothing else had. But again David
stood. He did not waver or falter. When he looked
at that enormous monster, I believe David saw right

through him to the lion and bear that God had caused him to conquer in times gone by. He did not give way to his senses or emotions; he based every movement on truth, focusing on the words of God that had been placed there in times gone by. He did not focus on the killer giant before him. He put his sights on the overcoming ability of God in him. Praise God for this incredible illustration in the Word of God that exemplifies the ability to overcome all fear with faith!

Lastly, there are priceless lessons to be learned from the beautiful Queen Esther. Esther was more than a radiant picture of authentic beauty and loveliness; she was a valiant heroine in the history of mankind. Although Esther unquestionably lived through her share of hardships, she refused to get stuck in victim mentality, and instead became an unparalleled model of strength. She is known as a mighty woman who saved a whole race of people through her selfless acts of bravery and obedience. There is much to be learned from the book of Esther. For now, you can focus on a few shining gems.

Raised in the home of her elder cousin Mordecai after being orphaned, Esther was a young Jewish girl going about her ordinary life when she was summoned to the king's palace. He was in search of a wife, and she was in the line-up. Esther's name means "star," and she indeed shone brightly in every way. She was truly lovely inside and out and found favor with all, including the king. He made her his wife.

Now a man called Haman was promoted by the king, and all the king's servants bowed to him except

Mordecai. This enraged Haman who plotted to destroy all the Jews. In obedience to Mordecai, Esther had withheld from the king all knowledge of her Jewish roots. Haman soon convinced King Ahasuerus that this group of people needed to be destroyed. Without realizing it, the king signed his wife's people over to the hands of the evil Haman and his plan to murder them. When Mordecai learned of the plan, he sent word to Esther and encouraged her to plead for mercy from the king on behalf of her native people.

Then Esther spoke to Hathach, and gave him a command for Mordecai: "All the king's servants and the people of the king's provinces know that any man or woman who goes into the inner court to the king, who has not been called, he has but one law: put all to death, except the one to whom the king holds out the golden scepter, that he may live. Yet I myself have not been called to go in to the king these thirty days." So they told Mordecai Esther's words.

And Mordecai told them to answer Esther; "Do not think in your heart that you will escape in the king's palace any more than all the other Jews. For if you remain completely silent at this time, relief and deliverance will arise for the Jews from another place, but you and your father's house will perish. Yet who knows whether you have come to the kingdom for such a time as this?"

Then Esther told them to reply to Mordecai: "Go, gather all the Jews who are present in Shushan, and fast for me; neither eat nor drink for three days,

*night or day. My maids and I will fast likewise. And
so I will go to the king, which is against the law; and
if I perish, I perish!" (Esther 4:10–14)*

Esther's initial hesitation and reluctance was certainly
justifiable. She would be risking the death penalty
by breaking the law and entering the king's court
uninvited. She was living in comfort for what might
have been the first time in her life, and she wasn't
jumping at the chance to mess it all up. Yet, destiny
itself summoned her in Mordecai's reply. Surely, a
fierce battle ensued between that divine destiny and
the terror that threatened to consume her. As Esther
made the difficult choice to close the door of fear
behind her, a relentless determination took over and a
door of favor and blessing opened wide.

*Now it happened on the third day that Esther put
on her royal robes and stood in the inner court of
the king's palace, across from the king's house, while
the king sat on his royal throne in the royal house,
facing the entrance of the house. So it was, when the
king saw Queen Esther standing in the court, that
she found favor in his sight, and the king held out to
Esther the golden scepter that was in his hand. Then
Esther went near and touched the top of the scepter.
(Esther 5:1–2)*

Without question, throughout that scenario, Esther
felt her heart beating wildly in her chest. It was the
moment of reckoning. Yet, she moved with purpose,
knowing that she had been chosen by God Himself
for this task. Not only did she have to shut out the
fear of inadequacy for such a moment, but she had to

overcome the fear of death itself. She shifted her focus to the favor of God and man that was with her. Instead of cowering in fear and staying in a place that felt safe, Esther slipped into the royal robes that she was made for and made a magnificent entrance.

Esther walked in wisdom even as her fears screamed at her. Rather than revealing everything right then and there, she simply invited the king and Haman to dinner. She had carefully planned a private banquet beforehand where she could humbly unveil her true request to the king. This exclusive invitation from the queen caused Haman to feel even more confident in his evil plans. At the advice of his family, he made gallows on which he planned to hang Mordecai the next day. Haman was completely unaware, but Queen Esther had traded her fear for a divine plan designed by the all-knowing God of the universe.

So the king and Haman went to dine with Queen Esther. And on the second day, at the banquet of wine, the king again said to Esther, "What is your petition, Queen Esther? It shall be granted you. And what is your request, up to half the kingdom? It shall be done!"

Then Queen Esther answered and said, "If I have found favor in your sight, O king, and if it pleases the king, let my life be given me at my petition, and my people at my request. For we have been sold, my people and I, to be destroyed, to be killed, and to be annihilated. Had we been sold as male and female slaves, I would have held my tongue, although the

enemy could never compensate for the king's loss"
(Esther 7:1–4).

Queen Esther went on to disclose to the king that the wicked Haman was the culprit behind this vicious plan. The king was enraged and had Haman hanged on the very gallows that had been prepared for Mordecai. The king then went on to promote Mordecai, who eventually became second in command to the king. Furthermore, he gave Mordecai and Esther the authority to reverse the edict set in place by Haman against the Jews. How might this have all ended if Esther had stayed in her royal comfort zone? May her determination and example inspire you to move beyond all fear to change history!

Along with those mentioned in this chapter, many others also faced monumental fear but chose to follow truth instead. These men and women were not supernatural in any way. They were people just like you. They heard lies of unworthiness and doubt just like you. They felt inferior, inadequate, and incapable. Still, they made the choice of faith to press through the fear and trust in the power of the Living God.

LET FAITH ARISE

Take this moment to reflect on areas of your life where you chronically deal with fear, worry, or anxiety. Consider the lies that keep you bound. Is it anxiety about tomorrow? God says He will care for you. Is it fear about the future of your children? He created them. They were His kids first. You are simply a vessel of love and guidance for Him to flow through. Is it fear of death? Your home is with Him. He has given you eternal life, and nothing can separate you from His love. Your life is not your own. He bought it with a price and He is careful to watch over you. Is it a fear of failure? He expects nothing of you other than complete trust in Him. When you seek and trust Him, you simply cannot fail in His eyes. On the contrary, He always causes you to triumph! Do you compare yourself to others and covet their gifts or abilities? He has blessed you with everything you need. He has chosen you! For every time you have a fearful thought, begin to turn it into faith-filled prayer. Take your fear to God in that moment and declare your trust in Him to make a way where you cannot see one!

Fears and lies come as a thief only to steal, kill, and destroy your life physically, emotionally, and spiritually. Jesus came for you to experience abundant life every day here and now on earth, not just in the life to come. For any fear that rises in your mind and heart, there is a blessed assurance in the Word of God that is more than able to put it to rest. Begin to turn those fears into faith as you trust the One and only Provider, Protector, Healer, and all-sufficient Source for every need in your life.

No matter where you have been, what you have done, or what horrific experiences you may have suffered through, with the help of the Holy Spirit, you can overcome any fear. As you draw nearer to Him each day, filling your heart and mind with more of Him and His truth, you will see that He is perfect love. As your life becomes penetrated with this perfect love, it will occupy every room of your heart and every crevice within your soul, leaving less and less room for fear. It simply cannot stay in the presence of the Almighty within you.

Deny the enemy any place of fear in your life. He only holds the power over you that you allow him to have. Discover all that God has for you as you put on your royal robes, pick up your slingshot, and step out of the boat. He will never, ever leave you!

chapter 7

FROM VICTIM TO VICTOR

Now thanks be to God who always leads us in triumph in Christ, And through us diffuses the fragrance of His knowledge in every place. ~ 2 Corinthians 2:14

THE BLAME GAME

Victory over life and the wiles of the devil are guaranteed in the life of the believer. If you believe and do not give up, you *will* overcome. Because of Jesus, losing is not an option unless you allow it to be. Meditating on this truth until it becomes revelation will transform how you look at life. It is sad, however, that many born again believers are still stuck in the miry mud of victim mentality. Through Jesus, God has made you an overcomer. Yet, it is impossible to walk as the overcomer that you are if you are focusing on all the wrong that has been done to you.

One of the most common signs of victim mentality is the act of blaming others. Your parents, siblings, spouse, children, and others in your life are not responsible for your happiness. You cannot control another person or his or her actions. You can, however, control yourself and your response. Whether you have been wronged, neglected, abused, mistreated, or unloved is irrelevant. That may sound harsh, but it is true. The circumstances of your past, present, or future are not responsible for your joy or lack thereof. Pure joy, true happiness, and real victory come from your inward condition, *not* your outward situation.

The placement of blame and victim mentality surfaced early in the history of humanity. Adam and Eve stepped right into the blame game in Genesis 3 after they disobeyed the instruction of the Lord.

Then the Lord called to Adam and said to him, "Where are you?"

So he said, "I heard Your voice in the garden, and I was afraid because I was naked; and I hid myself."

And He said, "Who told you that you were naked? Have you eaten from the tree of which I commanded you that you should not eat?"

Then the man said, "The woman whom You gave to be with me, she gave me of the tree, and I ate."

And the Lord God said to the woman, "What is this you have done?"

The woman said, "The serpent deceived me, and I ate"
(Genesis 3:9–13).

This is the ultimate example of the blame game that I am referring to. Adam was not exactly the bravest of men in this moment of vulnerability as he blamed his wife. It would have been much more respectable if he had just answered, "Yes, I ate of the tree you commanded me not to eat from." Although it was true that Eve had given him the fruit, it was also evident that he ate of his own accord. Eve followed right behind him by placing the blame on the serpent. Again, while it is true that the serpent deceived her, the fact remains that she acted of her own free will. Neither Adam nor Eve took personal responsibility for their actions. This is far too common in marriages, families, and ministries today.

The basis of victim mentality can be found in self-centeredness. If Adam had been more concerned with Eve's protection and well-being than his own, he would not have passed the baton of blame so quickly to her. In that moment of reckoning, however, he was more concerned with himself and his own image than he was about her. He believed the lie that he had been wronged and that someone else was to blame for his own actions. Eve proceeded to do the exact same thing, blaming the serpent for her own bad choice. Surely by that time she had realized the error of her ways. She had foolishly believed the serpent and disobeyed the directions of God. Clearly, each of them had taken part in the transgression, yet their self-centeredness kept them from taking any personal responsibility before the Lord.

PITY PARTY: YOU ARE INVITED

Self-pity is another common manifestation of victim mentality. The enemy of your life loves nothing more than to convince you to feel sorry for yourself. Misery truly does love company, and a life filled with self-pity will attract just that. Grumbling and complaining seems to draw the forces of darkness around you. Have you ever noticed that when you fall into murmuring and complaining you feel drained, lethargic, and just plain unhappy? Complaining does nothing to change your situation for the better, and it will steal your joy and the joy of those around you if it is tolerated in your life.

Thoughts of you being the only one who has problems, that no one cares, that you are not the best or favored one, that your life is miserable, or that everyone owes you something are all thoughts sent by Satan to steal your joy. The joy of the Lord is your strength according to Nehemiah 8:10. No wonder the enemy so desires to take it from you. You hold the power to let him or not. Do not fall for his lies that say you have every right to feel the way you do. Let go of every wrong and focus on everything Jesus did right. Look in the mirror and see the overcomer that God made you, not the victim that the enemy says you are.

The Israelites provide great insight into the power and destruction that can result from tolerating a victim mentality. They were delivered from the abusive hands of the Egyptians by the loving hand of God. Through Moses, God lead His chosen people out of a life of captivity and into a life of liberty. When the Egyptians realized what had happened, they began to pursue the Israelites in hopes of regaining them as slaves. Instead of trusting God in that moment, the Israelites gave way to fear and victim mentality.

When Pharaoh drew near, the Israelites looked up, and behold, the Egyptians were marching after them; and the Israelites were exceedingly frightened and cried out to the Lord.

And they said to Moses, Is it because there are no graves in Egypt that you have taken us away to die in the wilderness? Why have you treated us this way and brought us out of Egypt?

Did we not tell you in Egypt, Let us alone; let us serve the Egyptians? For it would have been better for us to serve the Egyptians than to die in the wilderness (Exodus 14:10–12 AMP, emphasis added).

Exodus 14 goes on to tell of how God miraculously parted the Red Sea for His people. After they were led out of Egypt, but before God parted the Sea for them, they actually asked to go back to their lives of captivity. Oftentimes people are most comfortable in their self-pity and do not desire to step out of the familiar prison of their bondage. It takes faith. Nothing less than full trust in God will move you out of the mindset of a victim into the life of the victor that you are. This is why it can be referred to as a miry muck. It is easy to get stuck there and miss out on an entire lifetime of joy, freedom, and victory.

Even in times of hardship and sickness, a person may unknowingly choose to stay in their situation because it is familiar to them. Perhaps they subconsciously enjoy the attention and pity they get from remaining bound to the situation they are in. This victim mentality can be an enormous hindrance to deliverance as it is in opposition to the will of God. The most effective way to walk in freedom and healing is to agree with God's will in the matter, and be willing to walk out of the situation even if it means moving into a place that is unfamiliar.

Exodus 15 goes on to describe great rejoicing among the people after God miraculously delivered them from bondage in Egypt. He parted the Red Sea so they could escape. How much more supernatural can something get? In that moment, they were thankful and sang to the Lord songs of praise and rejoicing. It did not take long, however, for complaining to set in once again.

So Moses brought Israel from the Red Sea; then they went out into the Wilderness of Shur. And they went three days in the wilderness and found no water. Now when they came to Marah, they could not drink the waters of Marah, for they were bitter. Therefore the name of it was called Marah. And the people complained against Moses, saying, "What shall we drink?" So he cried out to the LORD, and the LORD showed him a tree. When he cast it into the waters, the waters were made sweet (Exodus 15:22–25).

According to this account, it only took the Israelites three days to forget the amazing acts of God and get back into self-pity. Think about it for just a moment. These people had been harshly mistreated for generations. They had been slaves with no rights, no luxuries, and no confidence that their lives would ever amount to much. They had led oppressed and hopeless lives. They felt abused and devalued day in and day out. They were, indeed, victims of wrongdoing by the Egyptians. However, in this passage from Exodus, they had been made free by the Living God. They had seen His immense love for them through His miraculous deliverance of them. Yet, their victim mentality remained evident as they began to complain against Moses.

The Israelites did not just complain against Moses on one occasion, but over and over again. They were thirsty, they were hungry, or they did not like what the Lord provided for them. It was never good enough. They could never get past the mindset that they were mistreated and abused. That is how they saw themselves, and in turn, they lived in self-pity and defeat. If only they had stayed fixed on the great things God had done for them, things might have turned out differently. They would have had a different outlook when they spied out the land of Canaan as discussed earlier. They would have taken the land of plenty that God had intended for them and lived abundant lives there. Instead, they fixed their eyes on themselves and as a result, died in the wilderness, without ever seeing or tasting the magnificent things God had prepared for them in this life.

THE POWER OF PRAISE

Murmuring, complaining, and faultfinding will give place to negativity in your life. Praise and thanksgiving, on the other hand, will produce a bountiful harvest in your circumstances and life. Praise and thanksgiving are part of the language of God and angels. I believe you draw angels near when you lift your voice in gratitude toward God. You already know that the complaining and blaming that accompanies victim mentality depletes your joy. Worship does just the opposite. It fills your soul with gladness and causes a supernatural strength and peace to rise within you despite what is happening in your circumstances and the world that surrounds you.

Praise, worship, and thanksgiving do not always come easily. While your born-again spirit man is always rejoicing in the Lord, the outward man of flesh is warring to keep you in the trenches of self-pity, irritability, and selfishness. *You* determine who wins. As you set your sights on God, all He has done, and all He has planned for you, the enemy will flee.

Living a lifestyle of praise takes effort. Nothing about the Christian walk is passive. I am not saying that it involves striving for the approval of God, or that you do anything from your own strength. His yoke is easy, and His burden is truly light (Matthew 11:30). However, there is an effort to walking with purpose and faith. You must determine to remind yourself that you are an overcomer as opposed to a victim. Instead of focusing on the temporary afflictions of this life, focus on the things of God that are eternal (2 Corinthians 4:18). Trust the Lord and lean on His Holy Spirit throughout the day to help you walk as the victor He has made you!

RELEASING SHACKLES

Paul and Silas were imprisoned in Philippi and had every reason to complain. They were in a bad situation, and there appeared to be no way out. Yet, as they turned their eyes toward heaven, and chose praise over pain, the whole atmosphere shifted. The natural world was invaded with the power of the unseen realm of faith!

And when they had struck them with many blows, they threw them into prison, charging the jailer to keep them safely. He, having received [so strict a] charge, put them into the inner prison (the dungeon) and fastened their feet in the stocks. But about midnight, **as Paul and Silas were praying and singing hymns of praise to God,** *and the [other] prisoners were listening to them.* **Suddenly there was a great earthquake, so that the very foundations of the prison were shaken; and at once all the doors were opened and everyone's shackles were unfastened.** *When the jailer, startled out of his sleep, saw that the prison doors were open, he drew his sword and was on the point of killing himself, because he supposed that the prisoners had escaped. But Paul shouted, "Do not harm yourself, for we are all here!" Then [the jailer] called for lights and rushed in, and trembling and terrified he fell down before Paul and Silas. And he brought them out [of the dungeon] and said, Men, what is it necessary for me to do that I may be saved? And they answered, Believe in the Lord Jesus Christ [give yourself up to Him, take yourself out of your own keeping and entrust yourself into His keeping] and you will be saved, [and this applies both to] you and your household as well. And they declared the Word of the Lord [the doctrine concerning the attainment through Christ of eternal salvation in the kingdom of God] to him and to all who were in his house. And he took them the same hour of the night and bathed* *[them because of their bloody] wounds, and he was baptized immediately and all [the members of] his [household]. Then he took them up into his house and set food before them; and he leaped much for joy and exulted with all his family that he believed in God [accepting and joyously welcoming what He had made known through Christ] (Acts 16:23–34 AMP, emphasis added).*

The effects of praise and prayer from Paul and Silas not only loosed their own shackles, but the shackles of *all* the prisoners. It also empowered them to speak to the jailer, prevent him from committing suicide, and lead him and his household to the saving grace of Jesus. What an amazing example of the power of praise! Paul and Silas could easily have been caught up in feeling sorry for themselves, but instead they chose to focus on the faithfulness and ability of the God who had always come through for them before. What worked in the lives of Paul and Silas will work for you today!

Praise and prayer are powerful forces in our arsenal. Regardless of your situation, the mistreatment you may have suffered in the past, or what obstacles you may face daily, you are *not* a victim. Within you lies the power to move mountains. If you have the Spirit of Christ in you then you have the same power that caused Jesus to rise from the dead living on the inside of you (Romans 8:9–11)! With a little effort of faith on your part, shackles will be loosed, not only for yourself, but for prisoners around you as well.

Never be deceived into believing that no one else is watching. They are. It may be your child, spouse, parent, co-worker, or the clerk at the local market, but *someone* is watching and being influenced by your life. As you turn pity to praise and whining to worship, you will begin to see a difference in your own life and others will be drawn to you. Your circumstances may or may not change right away, but there will be a change within you that cannot be measured. Dare to praise Him today!

NO SMELL OF SMOKE

Shadrach, Meshach, and Abed-Nego truly went through a fiery trial as described in Daniel 3. They refused to bow to any false god. When they disobeyed the king and continued to honor God, the king became enraged and they were thrown in the fiery furnace. Witnesses saw a fourth man in the fire with them, and when they came out of the fiery furnace alive, everyone was amazed.

> *Then Shadrach, Meshach, and Abed-Nego came from the midst of the fire. And the satraps, administrators, governors, and the king's counselors gathered together, and they saw these men on whose bodies the fire had no power; the hair of their head was not singed nor were their garments affected, and the smell of fire was not on them* (Daniel 3:26–27).

How can someone go through a fire without being burned or even smelling like smoke? They were in the protective hands of the fourth man who walked through the fire with them. When you face difficulties in this life, you do not face them alone. The Lord walks with you; therefore, you can walk through your circumstance knowing you are walking *through* it instead of being consumed by it. When you cave to your fiery trial in terms of victim mentality, you will smell like smoke. Instead of diffusing the fragrance of Christ and His victory in your life, you will emit a pungent smell of defeat.

Have you ever heard a testimony from someone and been amazed at the things they have endured simply because there is no outward sign of their pain? I am talking about someone who has genuinely come through something horrific and yet they appear unscathed. They exude contentment and joy. I do not refer to someone who is faking it for the sake of a religious image. Sometimes things in this life are painfully difficult, and it is okay to admit it. But, I speak of a person who has truly walked through a fire and can still radiate the goodness of God. This is the picture of someone who is diffusing the fragrance of Christ. They do not revel in self-pity and give power to the pain, but they stand steadfastly in the faithfulness and power of Jesus.

Put your situation under your feet today. Declare the power of the Great I Am over your circumstance and praise Him even when you cannot see the way out. He will never leave you in the fiery furnace. He will always make a way out. Focus on Him and refuse to let His sweet fragrance in your life be replaced with the heavy stench of smoke.

GET OUT OF THE MIRY CLAY

As is the case with everything previously mentioned in this book, the choice is yours. Most people who have this mindset do not even realize it. They have focused for so long on the negative that they do not even notice what has happened. It is a stronghold that takes root and eventually takes over. Any stronghold can be familiar and keep you captive simply because it is comfortable to you.

Examine your life for a moment. Do you consistently look for someone to blame, even for the little things? Is it someone else's fault when you are having a bad day or when things go wrong? Are relationship issues always the fault of another? Do you let the little things get to you and ruin your attitude for the rest of the day? Do you find yourself thinking about how badly you are treated or have been treated in the past? Do you feel that people always owe something to you? These are all symptoms of victim mentality.

Focus on the overcomer that God says you are. Take ownership of your words and your actions toward others. Walk out of the comfort of your captivity and into true liberty. When you find yourself falling for the lies and believing you are a victim, stop and reflect on what God has said about you. Turn every thought of negativity, offense, and self-pity into thanksgiving, praise, and worship and see mountains move and shackles fall to the ground! He is forever faithful!

chapter 8

IT IS FINISHED!

So when Jesus had received the sour wine, he said, "It is finished!" And bowing His head, He gave up His spirit. ~ John 19:30

WHAT HAPPENED AT THE CROSS?

Most Bible believing Christians think they know all that happened at the Cross of Calvary. However, a close look at the Church proves something different. Far too many believers are consistently living in depression, defeat, poverty, sickness, and confusion. This is proof that a deeper revelation of the Cross is still needed. A more complete understanding of the all-sufficient work of Christ will open doors to abundance beyond anything you have ever known before.

When Jesus said, "It is finished!" He meant it. He didn't say, "It is almost finished." No, it was *completely* finished at the Cross. According to the Law, a blood

sacrifice was necessary for the remission of sin (Hebrews 9:22). Jesus came as the final and perfect sacrifice. There was no other sacrifice adequate enough
to make you right with God. He was it, and He was
perfect in every way.

The finished work at Calvary clearly included remission of sin. Every past, present, and future sin was
covered by the blood of the perfect Lamb. Only *He*
could remove every sin in your entire life as far from
you as the east is from the west, and He did. He did
not simply make a temporary sacrifice that would be
sufficient only until the next sin was committed. Indeed, that was how the Law worked, but the Law was
never what God had in mind as an eternal solution for
the redemption of mankind.

Far too many incorrect assumptions have been
made about God based on Old Testament Law. While
the Law was instituted by God to both constrain sin
that had become rampant and to reveal to mankind
their need for a Savior, it was *never* intended to be a
means of salvation. Yet, even today, it is often taught
as a requirement to become or to remain born again.
This could not be further from the truth!

*Is the Law then contrary and opposed to the
promises of God? Of course not! For if a Law had
been given which could confer [spiritual] life, then
righteousness and right standing with God would
certainly have come by Law.*

*But the Scriptures [picture all mankind as sinners] shut
up and imprisoned by sin, so that [the inheritance,*

blessing] which was promised through faith in Jesus Christ (the Messiah) might be given (released, delivered, and committed) to [all] those who believe [who adhere to and trust in and rely on Him].

Now before the faith came, we were perpetually guarded under the Law, kept in custody in preparation for the faith that was destined to be revealed (unveiled, disclosed),

So that the Law served [to us Jews] as our trainer [our guardian, our guide to Christ, to lead us] until Christ [came], that we might be justified (declared righteous, put in right standing with God) by and through faith.

But now that the faith has come, we are no longer under a trainer (the guardian of our childhood) (Galatians 3:21–25 AMP).

God was fully aware that mankind could never satisfy the Law without a Savior. Jesus Himself *fulfilled* the Law. This shows us that God never changed. He never changed His mind about the Law; He just made a way for it to be completely, eternally fulfilled through Christ. This reveals the true nature of God, which has always been and will always be love.

One of the most profound indications of the heart of God is evident in chapter three of Genesis, when God Himself made the first animal sacrifice of all as He compassionately clothed Adam and Eve. He also sent them from the Garden of Eden not to punish them, but to protect them and all who would come after them. Even in their sin and shame, God lovingly provided for Adam and Eve. Likewise, we were still sinners and without strength when Christ died for us (Romans 5:6). There is no greater love to be found. God did not wait for mankind to "get it together" before He sent His Son to make the ultimate sacrifice.

Now, by accepting the finished work of Jesus, you *become* the righteousness of God. This perfect exchange makes you as holy and righteous as Jesus in the eyes of God. Jesus was flawless and totally sinless, which is what made Him the perfect sacrifice. Yet, because of the joy that was before Him, He *became* sin so you could *become* righteous. *You*, my friend, were the joy set before Him! In His eyes, you were worth the suffering He had to endure.

Right standing with God came *fully* through the sacrifice of Jesus. This means you do not have to get born again over and over after every mistake, or even after an entire season of mistakes. I am *not* suggesting a lifestyle of sin. Sin will destroy your life, and it causes your heart to desensitize to the things of God. When you fail, it is critical that you take it to God and confess it to Him to keep your own conscience free from condemnation that causes you to believe there is separation between you and God. It is important to realize, however, that when you confess your sin to God, it is to keep *your* heart sensitive to Him and not to make Him accept you again. You are His beloved and you cannot earn His love and acceptance through right living or any self-effort. His acceptance of you is based *completely* on His Son.

There was a time in my life when I would go to the altar of the church for any and every altar call. I would beg God to forgive me and accept me. I repented during every church service and spent all my energy wondering if I could ever really become good enough to be acceptable to God. Honestly, I thought I was being humble. I lived under a heavy burden of condemnation, believing that I had everything to do with my worthiness in the eyes of my Heavenly Father. Thank God for the revelation from the Lord that He accepted me when *Jesus* made me acceptable! It was simply my job to receive it and walk in it. The day He revealed this to me, I was at a church service and the pastor asked for people to come up for prayer. It was for addictions, habits, and other issues. Then he asked for others to come up to form a line in front of those who had responded. He wanted these people to pray for those who were in need of prayer. I went forward for prayer that day.

Because of my constant consciousness of sin and unworthiness, I responded to the altar call. I went up and stood beside a young woman who was also there for prayer. I instantly felt impressed to pray for this woman, but I was in the same line as her and it was filled with people who would be prayed for by others. As the line of prayer ministers formed in front of us, I heard the question in my heart, "What are you up here for?" I couldn't answer. I was living wholeheartedly for the Lord. I did not have any known sin going on in my life. Yet, I still felt compelled to drag myself to the altar each and every time there was an invitation. Again, I heard the voice of the Lord softly speaking to my heart, "I wanted you to pray for the young woman you are standing beside. You are in the wrong line. I want to use you to minister freedom to others, but I cannot use you like this. You are more conscious of your own flaws than of the righteousness I have freely provided to you. You are using all of your energy to beg me for something I have already given to you. There is no energy left for you to give to others. You are focused on you, not Me." His words were not harsh, but they got the point through to my heart like a spear.

That day in the prayer line was a turning point for me. I am not suggesting that you get into pride and believe that you can never let anyone pray for you. We are the Body of Christ and scripture is clear that we are to pray for one another. On the contrary, neither should you believe the lie from the enemy that you are not perfect and therefore not usable. When you get a glimpse of the true grace of God, you will focus on His goodness and righteousness, and your life will forever change. Trying to earn your salvation or striving to hang on to your salvation based on your own merit is a vain attempt to be God of your own life. God is focused on the righteousness of Jesus in you, and you should be, too. Anything less cheapens the Cross and leaves you powerless!

The issue of sin was totally dealt with 2,000 years ago by Christ Jesus. This is the most miraculous gift of all. As amazing as it is, however, He did not stop there.

He was despised and rejected and forsaken by men,
a Man of sorrows and pains, and acquainted with
grief and sickness; and like One from Whom men

hide their faces He was despised, and we did not appreciate His worth or have any esteem for Him.

Surely He has borne our griefs (sicknesses, weaknesses, and distresses) and carried our sorrows and pains [of punishment], yet we [ignorantly] considered Him stricken, smitten, and afflicted by God [as if with leprosy].

But He was wounded for our transgressions, He was bruised for our guilt and iniquities; the chastisement [needful to obtain] peace and well-being for us was upon Him, and with the stripes [that wounded] Him we are healed and made whole (Isaiah 53:3–5 AMP).

The finished work of Jesus means even more than forgiveness of sins and eternal life in Heaven. Many Christians stop there. The truth is, however, that He provided everything we need for life and godliness (2 Peter 1:3). He became poor so you could be rich in every way. He was rejected so you could be accepted. He was wounded and broken so you could be healthy and whole in *every* area of life. Accept His gift of abundance in your spirit, physical body, and emotions. Nothing is missing and every good thing is available to you because of Jesus!

THE REAL YOU

Just as the enemy works to convince you of lies about God, he also works to convince you that you are not who God says you are. In reality, all that matters is what God says about you. It can take time to meditate on the Word of God and get it in your heart. The power and flow of God will be stifled in your life if you fail to realize who you are in Him and who He is in you. He lives in you, but will be able to flow most effectively through your life when you know your true identity.

Most believers are thankful just to be saved and going to heaven. They endeavor to lead good lives and be faithful in church attendance and service. Those are noble and good things, but let those same believers get a revelation of who they are in Christ, and they will elevate to new heights. They will become radical world-changers giving life to all that they touch. The minute you allow God Himself to take up residence on the inside of you, you accept your rightful position as a son or daughter of the Most High God. You are His, and life can be so much more than just status quo. I love how the following passage describes this new life:

> *This resurrection life you received from God is not a timid, grave-tending life. It's adventurously expectant, greeting God with a childlike "What's next, Papa?" God's Spirit touches our spirits and confirms who we really are. We know who he is, and we know who we are: Father and children. And we know we are going to get what's coming to us—an unbelievable inheritance! (Romans 8:15–17 MSG)*

The same passage in the NKJV says that you are "children of God" and "heirs of God and joint heirs with Christ." What an amazing truth! You are a son or daughter of God and brother or sister of Jesus! That is far different from being a beggar or lifeless, religious follower. It is *family*. It is a position of honor, and it is full of rights, promises, and love. You have a *right* to represent the Living God in all that you do and say. You are His child and you have His name engraved on your heart. If you were a king or queen, would you want your children to approach you as a mere servant, beggar, or stranger with no rights? Surely not! You would want them to know that they are yours and that they can have everything you have made available to them. Likewise, God yearns for you to approach Him as His child.

Let us then fearlessly and confidently and boldly draw near to the throne of grace (the throne of God's unmerited favor to us sinners), that we may receive mercy [for our failures] and find grace to help in good time for every need [appropriate help and well-timed help, coming just when we need it] (Hebrews 4:16 AMP).

It is nonsense and nothing short of deception for a believer to crawl to the altar in shame and condemnation as I did week after week. Instead, you can walk right up to your Father God at any given time, with any problem, failure, or need, and speak in boldness to Him about it. When you fail, thank Him for the provision of His mercy and forgiveness and move forward. Contrary to religious teaching, this brings Him pleasure. Allow *His* strength to work in you and through you to overcome any sin, habit, or hindrance you may be dealing with in your life. You do not have to fear His wrath or punishment since Jesus already took that upon Himself for you. Simply approach Him as your Daddy and enjoy the freedom you find there.

But you are a chosen generation, a royal priesthood, a holy nation, His own special people, that you may proclaim the praises of Him who called you out of darkness into His marvelous light; who once were not a people but are now the people of God, who had not obtained mercy but now have obtained mercy (1 Peter 2:9–10).

You have not been adopted by just anyone. You have been brought into the family of the King of all Kings! You are not a peasant; you are royalty. As such, you are royally and eternally blessed. Remember, this is not based on your goodness, but solely on the righteousness of Jesus. Do not accept a life of mediocrity or lack in *any* area when God Himself calls you highly favored and abundantly blessed!

Your position brings with it authority. It is crucial to recognize and walk in your God-given authority in order to have victory. If you are experiencing defeat in any area of your life, examine your beliefs on this topic. This is not an authority that has anything to do with your greatness, but *everything* to do with faith in the name of Jesus. Jesus clearly defines His authority and commands His followers to walk in it.

And Jesus came and spoke to them, saying, "All authority has been given to Me in heaven and on earth. Go therefore and make disciples of all the nations, baptizing them in the name of the Father and of the Son and of the Holy Spirit, teaching them

to observe all things that I have commanded you;
and lo, I am with you always, even to the end of the
age." Amen (Matthew 28:18–20)

Everything Jesus did in His ministry He did with
authority. He expects the same of you today. Passivity in this area means relegating your God-given authority to the devil, and it is dangerous. God desires
that you have faith in the name of Jesus and use it to
demonstrate His kingdom. In this broken world, you
are Jesus to the lost, hurting, and sick around you.
His chosen method to live in this world is in you and
through you. You are His temple and His vessel. This
is another change that occurred with the New Covenant of Grace. You and I became His chosen place
of residence. Now, whatever He accomplishes in this
world will be through His people. Gone are the days
of the Ark of the Covenant being moved from place
to place, and God living separate from His people.
No, His Spirit now dwells *within* His children as they
choose to abide in Him. You are His conduit. He desires to flow through you and to powerfully transform
lives around you as you submit to Him.

And these signs will follow those who believe: In
My name they will cast out demons; they will speak
with new tongues; they will take up serpents; and if
they drink anything deadly, it will by no means hurt
them; they will lay hands on the sick, and they will
recover (Mark 16:17–18).

Behold! I have given you authority and power to
trample upon serpents and scorpions, and [physical
and mental strength and ability] over all the power

that the enemy [possesses]; and nothing shall in any way harm you. (Luke 10:19 AMP)

Jesus clearly expressed His expectation for His followers to lead lives full of His power and authority. When you realize that this is who you are, you will find renewed strength to face this life. Every day will have new hope and new meaning. You will begin to live in confidence and bold expectancy instead of fear and self-consciousness. You will realize your purpose as you join with Him in accomplishing His perfect will in this world.

LIVING AS IF IT'S FINISHED

Do not believe the lie that you have no effective weapon to use against the attacks of the enemy. You are well equipped as a believer. Instead of living like God still has something to accomplish, focus on the finished work of the Cross. Jesus accomplished everything 2,000 years ago at Calvary. It was finished then and there for all time.

[God] disarmed the principalities and powers that were ranged against us and made a bold display and public example of them, in triumphing over them in Him and in it [the cross] (Colossians 2:15 AMP).

Every principality and power that rears its ugly head against you has already been disarmed by Jesus. Legalism, addiction, depression, sickness, and lack were all nailed to the cross. You do not have to wait on God, or beg Him to do something new in these areas. It is done. All that remains for you to do to see it manifest in the natural is to believe in what Jesus did and walk it out in faith. Stop begging God to see results in your life and instead speak victory to your situation. Speak out and believe all that Jesus did. The devil is a liar and does not want you to believe and stand on the finished work of Jesus. Defy Him by taking your rightful position and applying truth to every area of your life.

Imagine a prison door that has been unlocked. It is standing wide open with prisoners inside who have longed to go free. These prisoners, however, refuse to believe that the prison doors have been opened for them. As a result, they stay in their prison cell even though their pardon and freedom has been declared over them. Turn your eyes away from what experience has told you and look into the spiritual realm of faith today. See with the eyes of truth that your prison door has been opened and your day of pardon, freedom, and victory has come!

As a believer, you can live from a position of the finished work of Jesus. You can know in your heart and confidently declare over every storm of life that "It is finished!" Defeat, discouragement, sickness, lack, and all other works of the devil have been eternally finished! The devil and his lies must bow to the name of Jesus. Apply this revelation to your life and circumstances. Apply it to the doctor's report, your bank account, and any other negative thing that rises against you in this life.

Trust in the power of the Cross and all that was accomplished there. Faith in Jesus *will* produce results. Mountains will move and storms will cease in your life and the lives of those around you as you stand in that place of utter victory and boldly allow Him to live through you every minute of every day.

THE SUFFICIENCY OF GRACE

There is no greater gift than the grace of God. The measure of His gift is beyond anything you could ever ask or imagine. Christ's gift of becoming sin, taking your sickness, poverty, and pain of every kind, dying with it, and resurrecting in complete, unhindered freedom is more magnificent than the human mind can comprehend. What a beautiful, utterly complete, and selfless gift. And *you* have been given grace in accordance to the measure and magnitude of that gift!

> *Yet grace (God's unmerited favor) was given to each of us individually [not indiscriminately, but in different ways] in proportion to the measure of Christ's [rich and bounteous] gift (Ephesians 4:7 AMP).*

This means that for any given circumstance on any given day of your life, there is an abundance of grace to overcome. Regardless of the difficulty, pressure, or pain, His grace has already been given specifically and purposefully to you in direct proportion to what Christ gave. His gift is an eternal gift. It never runs out, it never leaves, and it never changes. His gift of Himself is all-sufficient. Therefore, the measure of grace given to *you* is all-sufficient, and you can draw on it every day of your life with every breath you take.

What a wonderful truth to realize! There will *always* be more grace than you will ever need to draw on in your life, because the gift Christ gave was an eternal river of abundant life. He invites you to drink from it unhindered, swim in it freely, and abide by it daily. This grace can never be measured or contained! His grace is enough to soothe any pain, mend any tear, and bridge any gap. Rest and rely on the immeasurable, impenetrable grace you have been freely given today! It is finished, indeed!

chapter 9

TAKING CHARGE

And from the days of John the Baptist until now the kingdom of heaven suffers violence, and the violent take it by force. ~ Matthew 11:12

YOU ARE THE DRIVER

Jesus did it all. It is true that He accomplished everything that needed to be accomplished for you to walk in freedom and victory. You do not have to look very far, however, to realize that a battle still rages. In this earth, Satan still roams about seeking those he may destroy through deception. A life of passivity will not bring forth the manifestation of victory that Jesus sacrificed to give you. *You* possess the power and authority to move Satan out of the driver's seat of your life through faith. You must take your victory by force!

While it is true that you are to rest in God, you must simultaneously walk in faith. To actively have faith through complete trust in Him, His finished work, His grace, faithfulness, and mercy *is* to rest in Him. Refuse to passively accept the lies of the enemy. Say, "No!" to sickness, defeat, and lack by agreeing with the Word of God in those areas. By doing so, you are taking charge of your life with the power of the truth of God.

> *The Lord is my Shepherd [to feed, guide, and shield me], I shall not lack. He makes me lie down in [fresh, tender] green pastures; He leads me beside the still and restful waters. He refreshes and restores my life (myself); He leads me in the paths of righteousness [uprightness and right standing with Him—not for my earning it, but] for His name's sake (Psalm 23:1–3 AMP).*

This world is full of restlessness. The economy, personal rights, and the fundamental morality of this world appear to all be in jeopardy. It is critical for you to realize that while the world around you may seem ominous and dark, there is a place where peace surpasses the confusion and still waters await you. It is a place of supernatural peace and shelter even in the midst of chaos.

Abiding in such a place doesn't just happen naturally. We must choose by faith to enter it (Hebrews 4:11). It is a process of learning to trust God completely, day by day, minute by minute. It means to completely rely on Him in the midst of any storm, no matter how dark.

There is an effort of faith on your part to get to and remain in that place when everything in the natural world looks and feels hopeless and uncertain. Again, I do not refer to striving to conjure up something that looks and sounds like faith. It is simply a decision of the heart to trust the God of peace and accept His every word as truth. This is a childlike faith and it brings forth mountain-moving results.

He who dwells in the shelter of the Most High will rest in the shadow of the Almighty. (Psalm 91:1)

You choose where you will dwell. As is customary with our Father, He does not force you to abide in His shelter and peaceful place of rest. If, however, you choose to dwell in the shadow of the Most High, you *will* find rest in His shadow. It doesn't happen by default just because you are a believer; it is a purposeful choice.

As you learn to put down your own self-reliance and lean on your loving, all-knowing Father, you enter a place of supernatural peace as He leads you beside still waters and quiets your soul as only He can. You can enter this secret place anytime, anywhere—at work, school, in the car, or in the midst of complete chaos. You can abide there knowing you are covered by His protective, loving wings—in the very shadow of the Almighty Creator of the universe! Where else would you ever want to be?

THE MIND AND THE MOUTH

My son, give attention to my words; Incline your ear to my sayings.

Do not let them depart from your eyes; Keep them in the midst of your heart;

For they are life to those who find them, And health to all their flesh. (Proverbs 4:20–22)

Learning to fully trust Him will result when you begin to meditate on the truth of His Word. Renewing your mind is a critical key to overcoming. Each chapter of this book is purposely filled with scripture. Use these and others for reflection and meditation. Dig into the Word of God and begin to eat it. It is food for your soul. It is life to your body. It is powerful, and it will produce results in your life!

For the Word that God speaks is alive and full of power [making it active, operative, energizing, and effective]; it is sharper than any two-edged sword, penetrating to the dividing line of the breath of life (soul) and [the immortal] spirit, and of joints and marrow [of the deepest parts of our nature], exposing and sifting and analyzing and judging the very thoughts and purposes of the heart (Hebrews 4:12 AMP).

According to 2 Corinthians 5:17, the minute you are born again you become a new creation. Your old spirit man is replaced with the living, perfect Spirit of God. Your soul is another matter, however. It consists of your mind, will, emotions, personality, etc. This is the place where most people live from. By that I mean that most people react to any given situation according to the state of their emotions, what they personally desire, or their random thoughts. While your spirit becomes new right away, your soul has some re-training to do. This is not an overnight process, but a continuous journey.

As you meditate on the Word of God and begin to implement it in your life, you will begin to think the thoughts of God and desire the things that He desires. You will begin to recognize thoughts that do not come from the heart of God, thoughts that are sent to deceive you and lead you astray.

And do not be conformed to this world, but be transformed by the renewing of your mind, that you may prove what is that good and acceptable and perfect will of God (Romans 12:2).

As you renew your mind, you will find yourself overcoming sin, habits, and addictions that once held you prisoner. This is why the concept of cleaning yourself up before you come to God is so futile. It is His truth and grace that set you free. You cannot do it in your own strength. As you renew your mind to His truth, you will find that you are able to take control of those thoughts that are sent to trap you, and you will learn to quickly replace them with the truth of God.

For though we walk (live) in the flesh, we are not carrying on our warfare according to the flesh and using mere human weapons. For the weapons of our warfare are not physical [weapons of flesh and blood], but they are mighty before God for the overthrow and destruction of strongholds,

[Inasmuch as we] refute arguments and theories and reasonings and every proud and lofty thing that sets itself up against the [true] knowledge of God; and we lead every thought and purpose away captive

into the obedience of Christ… (2 Corinthians 10:3–5 AMP).

Mind renewal is critical to living a triumphant life. It is the way to take control. Post scriptures everywhere you can. In my quest for freedom, I kept scriptures in the kitchen, the car, the bathroom, and everywhere that I would see them throughout the day.

Satan has used your mind as an entry point for years. It is where he enters to plant seeds of doubt, unbelief, confusion, discouragement, etc. If those thoughts are not taken captive, they will control your life. If they are replaced with truth, however, they will not stand a chance and your life will become a life of true prosperity. You will become an unshakeable force to reckon with.

Beloved, I pray that you may prosper in every way and [that your body] may keep well, even as [I know] your soul keeps well and prospers. (3 John 1:2)

Many people fail to recognize the importance of the relationship between the soul, spirit, and body. They are separate, yet very much connected. Your spirit man is as new and righteous as Jesus when you accept Him, but the soul and body are still stuck in their former life until you take over and get them in line with your renewed spirit. That only comes through the Word of God, time with Him, and the faithfulness of the Holy Spirit at work in your life. Empty scripture memorization and ritualistic prayers do not change your life. Again, God isn't looking for copycats. What works in my life or the life of someone else may not work for you. Find what works. If it is meditating on one verse a day that speaks to your heart, then meditate on it. It isn't about quantity; it is *all* about quality. You *will* see results. The Word of God is very much alive and all-powerful. When applied by faith, things will change.

So shall My word be that goes forth out of My mouth: it shall not return to Me void [without producing any effect, useless], but it shall accomplish that which I please and purpose, and it shall prosper in the thing for which I sent it (Isaiah 55:11 AMP).

As you fill your mind with truth, begin to change your words as well. Replace words of negativity, doubt, and fear with faith- filled words. Again, this is a process. Your tongue mixed with faith is a life-altering combination. It may sound strange at first, but put the faith of your heart and the truth of God's word to work with the words of your lips. Your words hold tremendous ability. Just as God created this world with His words and His words hold power, you also create with your words, and your words hold power. You are made in His image. Because His words have influence, so do yours.

Death and life are in the power of the tongue, And those who love it will eat its fruit (Proverbs 18:21).

Because he knows your words hold such potential, the enemy loves to control them. He accomplishes this by either keeping you silent or by convincing you that your words have no purpose. If he can convince you of the latter, you will let things come forth from your mouth that shouldn't, without even realizing what you have done. Every word you speak is like a seed sown in the field of your life and the lives of those around you. Words of faith, love, encouragement, and truth will bring forth a bountiful result of life-giving fruit in your life. Every negative word of doubt, criticism, jealousy, sarcasm, and anger will produce a weed or thorn that chokes out life. Words spoken with purpose and self-control bring life, peace, and joy. Your words matter.

It is time to move Satan out of the driver's seat of your life. Only you are able to do this by changing your mind and changing your words. As you do, your heart will change as well. Every thought and every word is either in agreement with your Father God or in agreement with the Father of Lies. As you become keenly aware of the power you possess and implement the wisdom of God, your life will be transformed, as will lives in your sphere of influence.

REMINDING YOUR SOUL

Why are you cast down, O my soul? And why are you disquieted within me? Hope in God, for I shall yet praise Him for the help of His countenance. (Psalm 42:5)

David spoke to his soul. He actually told his soul what to do and how to act. This may seem strange, but it is truly effective. Unlike the truth of God, your emotions are flighty. Your emotions are God-given and they are vital, but if left unchecked, they will control your life.

You are a three-part being: spirit, soul, and body (1 Thessalonians 5:23). Your soul consists of our mind, will, and emotions. You have already seen that once you are born again, your spirit is full of the Spirit of God, but oftentimes your soul lags behind. In your soul, you may become discouraged, frustrated, angry, and even depressed. It is in those times that you need to draw on your spirit man and the power of Christ in you to tell yourself what to do and how to act.

Speak to your soul with purpose. As you purpose to control your emotions instead of letting them rule your life and actions, you will begin to walk in greater victory and your emotions will experience a deeper degree of joy. While your mind, will, and emotions have their place of importance, they should be subject to your born-again spirit. As you renew your mind to the truth of the Word of God, this becomes easier.

Next time you wake up feeling grumpy, disgruntled, or down, take a moment to remind your soul of the greatness of your God. He is faithful, and He is your constant source of help. He never fails and never grows weary. You can count on Him in every situation. You need only to give thanks for it and remind your soul of the truth. Like David, you can speak to and quiet your soul with hope and praise for His faithfulness!

DESTINY: GREATNESS

The enemy of your soul knows that you were created for a purpose. That purpose may have been delayed or hidden from you by mistakes of the past, sin, or other obstacles, but it is still your purpose. One of the most life-changing messages I have ever heard was on this subject. My whole being illuminated when I realized that it was not too late for me to fulfill my purpose. The enemy had convinced me that because of my past, even though I was living for the Lord, I could not be a minister of the gospel of grace and reconciliation.

Even with many years gone by, the desire of my heart to minister truth was just as alive as it had been when I was the bold little girl of days gone by. My passion and desire to partner with God and change the world around me was still strong. I knew I was called, but I had listened to the lie that I had missed my opportunity. When I heard the truth that my purpose remained, I rejoiced and began to walk in it once again. I experienced a new level of confidence, hope, and expectancy.

There are many examples in scripture of those who moved beyond their humanity to live their lives for God. They changed history and proved what a radical faith in God can accomplish in the life of an ordinary human being. These men and women were no different from you. Abraham comes to mind as one who defied the natural to walk in the supernatural in this world.

Therefore it is of faith that it might be according to grace, so that the promise might be sure to all the seed, not only to those who are of the law, but also to those who are of the faith of Abraham, who is the father of us all (as it is written, "I have made you a father of many nations") in the presence of Him whom he believed—God, who gives life to the dead and calls those things which do not exist as though they did; who, contrary to hope, in hope believed, so that he became the father of many nations, according to what was spoken, "So shall your descendants be." And not being weak in faith, he did not consider his own body, already dead (since he was about a hundred years old), and the deadness of Sarah's womb. He did not waver at the promise of God through unbelief, but was strengthened in faith, giving glory to God, and being fully convinced that what He had promised He was also able to perform. And therefore "it was accounted to him for righteousness" (Romans 4:16–22).

Abraham did not budge when it came to trusting the Lord. As you already know, he failed to do it all perfectly, but what a difference his life made! It would have been easy to stay in his comfort zone. He had a comfortable life, yet he left it all behind to follow the voice of God.

By faith Abraham obeyed when he was called to go out to the place which he would receive as an inheritance. And he went out, not knowing where he was going. By faith he dwelt in the land of promise as in a foreign country, dwelling in tents with Isaac and Jacob, the heirs with him of the same promise; for he waited for the city which has foundations, whose builder and maker is God.

By faith Sarah herself also received strength to conceive seed, and she bore a child when she was past the age, because she judged Him faithful who had promised. Therefore from one man, and him as good as dead, were born as many as the stars of the sky in multitude—innumerable as the sand which is by the seashore (Hebrews 11:8–12).

Noah, too, was a faith-filled world changer. He must have looked like an idiot to those around him. He was building a huge boat even though a flood had never been heard of among the people. It would have been so tempting to listen to the sneers and jeers and back out of his deal with God just to save face with his neighbors and friends. Instead, he faithfully built day after day until he accomplished the thing God had asked of him.

[Prompted] by faith Noah, being forewarned by God concerning events of which as yet there was no visible sign, took heed and diligently and reverently constructed and prepared an ark for the deliverance of his own family. By this [his faith which relied on God] he passed judgment and sentence on the world's unbelief and became an heir and possessor of righteousness (that relation of being right into which God puts the person who has faith) (Hebrews 11:7 AMP).

Think of the apostle Paul. His dark past probably far surpasses anything you or I have done. He murdered Christians and enjoyed it. It is probably safe to assume that Satan came to him after his encounter with Jesus to try and steal from him. He probably tried to convince him that he was of no use in the kingdom of God since he had committed such horrific sins. Surely he whispered to him that he had missed his opportunity and would never be fit for kingdom purpose no matter how much his heart had changed. Yet, Paul went on to walk in the world-changing destiny to which he had been called.

What about Noah, Daniel, David, Rahab, Esther, Moses, and Sarah? These are only a few of the history makers named in the Bible. They all had a choice just like you. They pressed through lies about their inadequacies, worthlessness, fear, age restrictions, physical impossibilities, and less than perfect lineage to walk in the divine destiny to which they were called. They were created for something great, and they knew it. They felt it in the depths of their soul and mediocrity simply would not satisfy.

Notice that God does not implement age limits. Some of the greatest feats in the history of mankind were achieved by people who might be considered the "older generation." It is not acceptable to use your age as a measuring tool for your purpose or for an excuse to sit down and rock until you pass from this life to the next. Regardless of age or spiritual maturity, you never "arrive" in this life. God is always doing something new in your life and heart. He wants to partner with you and walk with you right where you are. Whether you are on a playground preaching to your 2nd grade peers, in your 90s imparting love and encouragement to those in your sphere of influence, or somewhere in between, you are His and you are useful! He never discards His own. He only moves you from glory to glory. Here is what God has to say about old age:

The [uncompromisingly] righteous shall flourish like the palm tree [be long-lived, stately, upright, useful, and fruitful]; they shall grow like a cedar in Lebanon [majestic, stable, durable, and incorruptible].

*Planted in the house of the Lord, they shall flourish
in the courts of our God.*

[Growing in grace] **they shall still bring forth fruit
in old age; they shall be full of sap [of spiritual
vitality] and [rich in the] verdure [of trust, love,
and contentment].**

**[They are living memorials] to show that the Lord
is upright and faithful to His promises;** *He is my
Rock, and there is no unrighteousness in Him (Psalm
92:12–15 AMP, emphasis added).*

The world may not look at the older generation with
much honor, but God says you are vitally important.
You do not have to settle for a broken down life. Instead,
wake up each day with thankfulness on your tongue.
Believe the words of the Lord. Bring forth fruit and be
full of spiritual vitality. You are a living memorial to
everyone around you of the goodness and faithfulness
of God. Never give up!

HIS PLANS

You were called for something bigger than you can ever
do in your own strength. It is not about your natural
ability, the perfection of your past, or how badly you
may have blown it. It is all about what God says about
you. No one is called or worthy based on those merits.
God has had a special purpose in mind for you since
before time began.

*For we are God's [own] handiwork (His work-
manship), recreated in Christ Jesus, [born anew]*

that we may do those good works which God
predestined (planned beforehand) for us [taking
paths which He prepared ahead of time], that we
should walk in them [living the good life which
He prearranged and made ready for us to live].
(Ephesians 2:10 AMP)

Plans and circumstances may change. Life is full of changes. Your life may look far different from how you once envisioned that it would turn out. People change. None of it matters when it comes to the purpose God has for your life. Your purpose in Christ remains and so does His faithfulness to empower you to walk in it.

What is the dream of your heart? Do you remember a desire or passion that you once had that has been stifled by the cares of this world? Ask the Lord to show you that seed that He planted in your heart, and to plant new seeds of purpose as well. Break out of the molds of this temporary world and into the world of the radical destiny that He has planned for you. It will be beyond anything you have dreamed!

You were fashioned for greatness. Mediocrity simply is *not* in your born again DNA. Determine in your heart to resist the devil and his lies. Stand on the truth of God's Word and agree with what He says about you. Begin to walk in the plans that He has ordered for your life one step at a time. Trust Him with all of your heart. Lay your past at His feet, and put your future in His hands as you walk into the destiny He has crafted especially for you. You are His beloved son or daughter. Never believe anything less about yourself or about His great love for you. This is the first day of the rest of your life. Don't waste another moment of time believing the lies of Satan. Walk in truth and live forever free!

CONCLUSION

My intention throughout this book has been to share truths that stir up your faith so you might clearly see areas of your life where you may have believed lies from the enemy. He seeks to destroy you, and the defense you have against him is truth. Revelation I have shared with you has come from God's Word, where you will find every answer and principle of wisdom you will need in this life. I have included several other scriptures in these final pages of the book. The Bible is full of priceless gems just waiting for you. Search for them as if you are searching for priceless treasure. They make your life richer, and they fill you with wisdom. The Lord is not hiding anything from you or withholding any good thing from you. In contrast, every good and perfect gift comes from Him (James 1:17). When you seek Him, you will find Him (Jeremiah 29:13).

As one of the scriptures that follows urges, you should "taste and see that the Lord is good." Others can tell you how wonderful it is, but only *you* can bring the cup to your lips and taste it for yourself. I pray that the words that you have read within this book have caused you to thirst for more of the truth from God.

His living water will quench the thirst within you and fully satisfy your soul. In closing, the prayer of my heart for you is this:

"... that the God of our Lord Jesus Christ, the Father of glory, may give to you the spirit of wisdom and revelation in the knowledge of Him, the eyes of your understanding being enlightened; that you may know what is the hope of His calling, what are the riches of the glory of His inheritance in the saints, and what is the exceeding greatness of His power toward us who believe, according to the working of His mighty power which He worked in Christ when He raised Him from the dead and seated Him at His right hand in the heavenly places, far above all principality and power and might and dominion, and every name that is named, not only in this age but also in that which is to come" (Ephesians 1:17–21).

With love,

Jill

SCRIPTURES FOR MEDITATION

THE LOVE AND GOODNESS OF GOD:

For I am persuaded that neither death nor life, nor angels nor principalities nor powers, nor things present nor things to come, nor height nor depth, nor any other created thing, shall be able to separate us from the love of God which is in Christ Jesus our Lord (Romans 8:38–39).

The Lord your God in your midst, The Mighty One, will save; He will rejoice over you with gladness, He will quiet you with His love, He will rejoice over you with singing. (Zephaniah 3:17)

Oh, taste and see that the Lord is good; Blessed is the man who trusts in Him! (Psalm 34:7)

HE MADE YOU AND SEALED YOU:

In Him you also trusted, after you heard the word of truth, the gospel of your salvation; in whom also, having believed, you were sealed with the Holy Spirit of promise (Ephesians 1:13).

For we are God's [own] handiwork (His workmanship), recreated in Christ Jesus, [born anew] that we may do those good works which God predestined (planned beforehand) for us [taking paths which He prepared ahead of time], that we should walk in them [living the good life which He prearranged and made ready for us to live] (Ephesians 2:10 AMP).

Before I shaped you in the womb, I knew all about you. Before you saw the light of day, I had holy plans for you: A prophet to the nations—that's what I had in mind for you (Jeremiah 1:5 MSG).

YOU ARE HIS CHILD:

But as many as received Him, to them He gave the right to become children of God, to those who believe in His name: who were born, not of blood, nor of the will of the flesh, nor of the will of man, but of God (John 1:11).

Behold what manner of love the Father has bestowed on us, that we should be called children of God! (1 John 3:1a)

For you are all sons of God through faith in Christ Jesus (Galatians 3:26).

FORGIVENESS:

Let all bitterness, wrath, anger, clamor, and evil speaking be put away from you, with all malice.

And be kind to one another, tenderhearted, forgiving one another, even as God in Christ forgave you (Ephesians 4:31–32).

But I say to you, love your enemies, bless those who curse you, do good to those who hate you, and pray for those who spitefully use you and persecute you ... (Matthew 5:44).

Be gentle and forbearing with one another and, if one has a difference (a grievance or complaint) against another, readily pardoning each other; even as the Lord has [freely] forgiven you, so must you also [forgive] (Colossians 3:13).

OVERCOMING FEAR:

Peace I leave with you; My [own] peace I now give and bequeath to you. Not as the world gives do I give to you. Do not let your hearts be troubled, neither let them be afraid. [Stop allowing yourselves to be agitated and disturbed; and do not permit yourselves to be fearful and intimidated and cowardly and unsettled.] (John 14:27 AMP).

Since we have such [glorious] hope (such joyful and confident expectation), we speak very freely and openly and fearlessly (2 Corinthians 3:12 AMP).

For as many as are led by the Spirit of God, these are sons of God. For you did not receive the spirit of bondage again to fear, but you received the Spirit of adoption by whom we cry out, "Abba, Father" (Romans 8:14–15).

For God has not given us a spirit of fear, but of power and of love, and of a sound mind (2 Tim. 1:7).

YOUR SUFFICIENCY IN CHRIST:

I can do all things through Christ who strengthens me (Philippians 4:13).

But God, who is rich in mercy, because of His great love with which He loved us, even when we were dead in trespasses, made us alive together with Christ (by grace you have been saved), and raised us up together, and made us sit together in the heavenly places in Christ Jesus, that in the ages to come He might show the exceeding riches of His grace in His kindness toward us in Christ Jesus (Ephesians 2:4–7).

Blessed be the God and Father of our Lord Jesus Christ, who has blessed us with every spiritual blessing in the heavenly places in Christ, just as He chose us in Him before the foundation of the world, that we should be holy and without blame before Him in love, having predestined us to adoption as sons by Jesus Christ to Himself, according to the good pleasure of His will, to the praise of the glory of His grace, by which He made us accepted in the Beloved (Ephesians 1:3–6).

MOVING AHEAD:

But as it is written: "Eye has not seen, nor ear heard, Nor have entered into the heart of man The things which God has prepared for those who love Him" (1 Corinthians 2:9).

Now to Him Who, by (in consequence of) the [action of His] power that is at work within us, is able to [carry out His purpose and] do superabundantly, far over and above all that we [dare] ask or think [infinitely beyond our highest prayers, desires, thoughts, hopes, or dreams] (Ephesians 3:20 AMP).

Do not remember the former things, Nor consider the things of old. Behold, I will do a new thing, Now it shall spring forth; Shall you not know it? I will even make a road in the wilderness, And rivers in the desert (Isaiah 43:18–19).

I'm not saying that I have this all together, that I have it made. But I am well on my way, reaching out for Christ, who has so wondrously reached out for me. Friends, don't get me wrong: By no means do I count myself an expert in all of this, but I've got my eye on the goal, where God is beckoning us onward—to Jesus. I'm off and running, and I'm not turning back (Philippians 3:13–14 MSG).

He shall be like a tree, Planted by the rivers of water, That brings forth its fruit in its season, Whose leaf also shall not wither; And whatever he does shall prosper (Psalm 1:3).

STUDY GUIDE

This guide is full of questions that will foster discussion and thought whether you are using it in a classroom, church, small group, or your own personal study. It is a tool to be used alongside the book and as the Holy Spirit leads.

If you are using this in a group setting remember, it is not about right or wrong answers. This isn't a test; it is a tool. Everyone may not agree on every point. Let the Holy Spirit and the love and Word of God direct you.

"As iron sharpens iron, so a friend sharpens a friend." (Proverbs 27:17) Learning, growth, and revelation flow from these types of discussions. Occasionally a question may be too personal for some people to comfortably discuss in a group. That's okay. The Holy Spirit is still at work.

Here are some ideas for using this guide in a group setting:

1) Read a chapter of the book. This can be done individually or together in a group setting.

2) Use the questions corresponding to each chapter in this guide to have meaningful discussions about what you read. You can also have group

members complete the questions for the chapter ahead of time and then discuss answers and thoughts together.

3) Pray together and for one another. Find scriptures to stand on for specific needs. Believe God and agree with His Word over one another.

4) Encourage one another to walk in what you have learned. Apply it to your life and encourage others to do the same. This will produce fruitfulness in your life.

May this guide be a blessing to you and help you lead others into a whole new dimension of freedom and victory!

CHAPTER 1 – DISCUSSION QUESTIONS

• According to Ephesians 3:1-6 (MSG), what have God's intentions been for you since before the world was formed?

• What was your relationship with your earthly father like and how do you think it has affected you and your image of God?

• How does knowing God's heart toward you make a difference in your life?

• I mention in the book that God's heart is your true spiritual home – your place of origination. Explain what that means to you.

- In contrast to God's intentions for you, Satan wants to lure you away from your true spiritual home (your Father's heart). Share some examples of these thoughts and mindsets that he has used in your life to attempt to lure you away from truth.

- Read Revelation 12:11. I share about the prodigal son and about my own experience of "coming to my senses." Is there a time in your life when you awakened to truth? Briefly share your experience.

- Do you think sharing your experience as a testimony could be helpful to anyone else? Explain your answer.

- Why do you think it important to have an accurate image of God?

- Truthfully describe what you believe God is like and explain how you believe it has impacted your life and intimacy with Him.

- Using Hebrews 11:6, 1 John 4:8-9, John 10:10 and 1 Corinthians 13:4-8, describe God's nature in a few words.

CHAPTER 2 – DISCUSSION QUESTIONS

- Why does Satan want you to believe that women are less important than men in God's eyes?

- How has this lie impacted the Body of Christ as a whole?

- Whether you are a man or woman, share how the enemy has tried to perpetrate this subtle lie in your life – in your relationships, church, ministry, workplace, or in your own thoughts. Give examples.

- According to Genesis 1:26-27, who was made in the image of God?

- Describe God's heart and attitude toward women according to Genesis 1:26-27 and Galatians 3:28.

- Read Genesis 12:10-20. From this passage, I shared about two reasons for God's favor, protection, and provision that followed Abraham (Abram) even in the midst of his failure. What were they?

- Hagar was a slave and not God's first choice for Abraham's seed. Why do you think He pursued her when she fled?

- Reflect and share about how God has pursued you in your life and circumstances.

- What qualified Rahab to become part of the lineage of Christ?

- How did Jesus convey His Father's heart for women during His earthly ministry? Share examples.

CHAPTER 3 – DISCUSSION QUESTIONS

- Can men be plagued by brokenness, emotional sickness, insecurity and self-doubt? Explain.

- Share examples of traps the enemy might set specifically for men.

- What transformed Zacchaeus as he dined with Jesus?

- Where do words of insignificance over your life come from?

- Is it possible for God to fill the void caused by the absence, neglect, or abuse of an earthly father? Explain your answer.

- Why is it so important for a man to get his sense of worth and acceptance from God?

- How can hidden, unhealed wounds affect people close to you? Share examples.

- Was it David's spotless life and great business accomplishments that qualified him as "a man after God's own heart?" Explain your answer.

- According to Genesis 1:26-28, who was created to rule, subdue, and have dominion? Did that include dominion over one another? Explain.

- In your own words explain how domination differs from headship.

CHAPTER 4 – DISCUSSION QUESTIONS

- How can unforgiveness hinder a life of victory?

- Is it possible to have bitterness in your heart without realizing it? Explain your answer.

- Explain how you can forgive from your spirit but not "feel" it in your emotions.

- How is it possible for someone to come in the name of the Lord and not accurately represent the heart of the Lord?

- In your own words, explain how forgiveness is a choice.

- What blessings did Joseph experience in his life as a result of choosing to forgive?

- Does forgiving someone mean you must trust them? Explain your answer.

- Why is it important to forgive yourself? Explain your answer.

- Is there any sin that you have compartmentalized as "unforgiveable"?

- Is there anyone in your life, including yourself, whom you have failed to forgive? If so, take the time NOW to lay it at the feet of Jesus. The burden is not for you to carry. It is His.

CHAPTER 5 – DISCUSSION QUESTIONS

- Has the enemy ever tried to convince you that you were not as valuable as others? Explain.

- Explain why your thought life is so powerful.

- After reading Numbers 13:26-33 explain how thoughts kept the Israelites from entering the Promised Land.

- In contrast to the thoughts of the other ten spies, what did Caleb and Joshua see according to Numbers 14:6-8?

- Describe how you see yourself.

- What makes us worthy in the eyes of God? Explain.

- Explain false humility vs. true humility.

- Have you or someone you know ever felt that it was "too late" to be used by God? Explain.

- How did Peter fail when Jesus was arrested, and what did he go on to accomplish later in Acts 1:15, Acts 2:38-41, and Acts 3:2-7?

- What thoughts of worthlessness can you "weed out" today in order walk more fully in the purpose God has for you?

CHAPTER 6 – DISCUSSION QUESTIONS

- What are some of the forms of fear discussed in the book?

- What physical effects can fear cause?

- Have you or someone you know ever allowed fear to keep you from doing something you felt the Lord prompting you to do?

- According to Judges 4:4-10, what did Barak give up as a result of submitting to fear?

- In 1 Samuel 17:31-37, what thoughts did David focus on that gave him the courage to believe he could defeat Goliath?

- Explain how Esther had to overcome fear in order to fulfill the will of God in her life and situation.

- Identify areas of your life where you chronically deal with fear.

- List some practical ways to deal with fear when it comes against you.

- What is the purpose behind fear?

- Identify some scriptures that deal with the particular fears you face on an ongoing basis. Use these scriptures (read them, meditate on them, write them, and speak them) until truth is more real to you than the fear you face.

CHAPTER 7 – DISCUSSION QUESTIONS

- Can you walk as an overcomer if you are identifying yourself as a victim? Explain.

- Why is it that your circumstances (past, present, or future) are ultimately not connected to your level of joy?

- Explain how Adam and Eve fell into the trap of victim mentality and the "blame game" in Genesis 3.

- What does grumbling and complaining accomplish?

- Have you ever chosen thanksgiving and praise over grumbling and complaining in a difficult situation? Share the results.

- How is it possible for a negative situation or stronghold to become familiar and comfortable?

- Explain how victim mentality and self-pity can hinder deliverance, healing, and breakthrough in a situation.

- Why is it so important to focus on the eternal things of God rather than the temporary situations of this life?

- Is it possible to pass through a proverbial "fire" and not smell like smoke? Explain.

- Identify areas in your life where you may be exhibiting victim mentality or may have become comfortable in a situation sent by the enemy. Choose to thank God for victory over that situation and begin to walk free!

CHAPTER 8 – DISCUSSION QUESTIONS

- Explain what Jesus meant when He proclaimed, "It is finished."

- Explain why Jesus was the perfect and only acceptable sacrifice for our sin.

- Explain how Jesus fulfilled the law. What is the significance of that?

- Why did Jesus send Adam and Eve out of the Garden of Eden? How does that indicate His heart for His children?

- How is it possible to become the righteousness of God?

- What do you believe God says about you? (Be specific.)

- Do your works cause you to be accepted by God? Explain.

- What does it mean to you that we are "heirs of God and joint heirs with Christ"?

- What does it mean to you that you can boldly approach God's throne of grace?

- According to Colossians 2:15, what did Jesus do to the principalities and powers that rise against us?

CHAPTER 9 – DISCUSSION QUESTIONS

- What does it mean to you to take your victory by force?

- How is resting in God actually an act of faith?

- Why is passivity dangerous?

- What does it mean to "dwell in the shelter of the Most High" and "rest in the shadow of the Almighty"?

- According to 2 Corinthians 5:17, what happens when you are born again?

- Why does your soul need to be re-trained or renewed?

- Why are your words important?

- What does it mean to "remind your soul" and why is it necessary?

- Do you believe you were created on purpose, with purpose, and for a purpose? Explain your answer.

- Dust off the dreams God has placed in your heart. Write them down and ask God how He wants them to come to pass in your life. This is the very first day of the rest of your life!

PRAYER OF SALVATION

If you would like to make Jesus the Lord of your life by accepting all that He has abundantly provided for you, believe in your heart as you pray this prayer:

Lord Jesus, thank you for loving me, dying on the cross for me, and making it possible to be fully and completely forgiven of my sin—past, present, and future. I believe that You were the perfect sacrifice and that you died, rose from the dead, and are alive now and forever. I accept and thank you for Your completely finished work, and for making me Your joint heir. I accept your free and all sufficient gift of grace right now. Amen.

PLEASE CONTACT US

If this book has impacted your life, you have accepted all that Jesus has done by praying the prayer above, or you have some other testimony to share, we would love to hear from you! Please send an email to *testimony@ transcendministries.org* or write to:

Transcend Ministries, Inc.
P.O. Box 7911
Woodland Park, CO 80863

www.transcendministries.org